LIVING (and eating), DELIBERATELY

Food, family, philosophy; Ikarian Style

Dianna Lefas

LIVING (and eating), DELIBERATELY

LIVING (and eating), DELIBERATELY

Dedicated to my parents
Philipos & Clairesunday Lefas,
My beloved Aunt Xie Papadakis
And my grandparents Elias (Louis) & Demetria,
And Georgios & Eleni
And to every single Ikarian who knew they
could make a robust living out of a rock.

LIVING (and eating), DELIBERATELY

Perdiki Publishing

Cover photograph by Alethea Brown Kniffen
(photograph: from the southeast shore of Ikaria
across the Aegean Sea).

LIVING (and eating), DELIBERATELY

TABLE OF CONTENTS

Chapter One

IKARIAN WAYS – AN INTRODUCTION

"If you see an Ikarian running, then his house is on fire."

"The only ones awake during siesta are foreigners and crazy people."

When I first laid eyes on the Aegean, a crystal blue that hummed under a steaming, transparent azure sky, and the miles of glistening Ikarian beaches reflecting off shimmering white buildings that seemed to explode under the sun like erratic camera flashes, my first instinct was to put on sunglasses. After muting the glare, I looked again. Here it was that I came face to face with my past as well as my present.

I thought that the oral history of my people and the old masters of philosophy could be my tools to a deeper understanding of who I was. But, in an odd way, the first gleam of embryonic understanding came from the one commonality that sustains the whole of the human race – food.

As a chef, my father's connection to food was not merely a working relationship; it was a romantic attachment to the rhythm of life, a celebratory enactment of a reverence about which I was soon to learn. It was while in Greece, among the wild poppies and olive groves, that I learned the mystery of food and how it entwined itself intimately in the story of the human race. There was a specific food to celebrate the birth of a child, a specific food to mourn the loss of a loved one and a specific food to remember that the dead shall one day rise again. The food is Koliva; boiled wheat, symbolic of life and the hope of resurrection – anabiosis.

For my parents, my father especially who was never far removed from the island of his birth, life was for truly living. That was his philosophy. Like his fellow islanders, my father was very laid back. He did not plot his tomorrows. In America, not plotting for your future is like hanging yourself, because there is a need to keep pace with those around you or you will find yourself left far behind. For my father and islanders like him, stressing over tomorrow was such a foreign abstract (which explains the Ikarians' fondness for tardiness), because all his life he, and his parents and grandparents before him, had been groomed to live in the moment. The hardships of life; the unexpected tragedies from which they could not readily flee because they were isolated on an island; 7,000 years of pirate raids, hostile takeovers and foreign occupations, taught them that tomorrow had no guarantees, and that if you didn't grasp tightly to the moment you were in, you stood a good chance of losing it all.

The philosophy is simple: You never own tomorrow – the only thing you possess with certainty is the moment you are in – and so you learn to make the absolute most of it, to live with all the deliberate, robust vitality you can muster. This is not only a good idea – it's an inheritance. Tomorrow you may die. Right now, however, you may dance. And dine. And love. Right now. This 'now' is the moment in which to exercise your full and alert senses and appreciation for everything around you, to relish the wide vibrancy of life. Exactly now. It's called "living deliberately" – living with focus and intent. Living, as in not so much "doing," but "being." Living with eyes and heart wide open. It's enjoying your friends' smiles, savoring the aromatic flavor of the food before you, appreciating the bouquet of the wine

With your entire being, allowing the sun and water and floral scents to make an indelible mark upon your soul. And the music! – feeling your body absorb the notes, the rhythm, the laughter, the love of all things beautiful. Setting your feet firmly on the ground and feeling the steadiness of the ground under you. And knowing that tomorrow is not ever a good time to say I love you, when you could say I love you right now. Waiting is simply a waste of a fragile and unpredictable filament of time that never repeats itself and that you could never get back. And though sitting around wining and dining might seem like a leisurely waste of time, it can be productive when you tell someone, whoever it is, not what's wrong with them - which is often too easy to do – but what's right with them. This is life affirming and part of living deliberately.

There is another factor to living deliberately – and better. My father, as his mother, sisters, brothers and many of the people I knew on the island, had one aspect that seemed, to me, more pronounced than the others. He forgave immediately. He was not one to hold a grudge. And, thinking about it, that would have to be part of the survival mechanism on the island, for if people held grudges with everyone who hurt them, it would turn into a very small island, indeed. As it is, the island is only twenty-five miles long and around five miles wide. There really is no place to hide if you want to isolate yourself from those against whom you are harboring resentment. Unless the transgression was grossly egregious, the most intelligent and freeing thing one could do was to simply forgive. The stress this eliminates is massively important for the heart, blood pressure, immune system, and mental and spiritual health.

One prime example of this was the one day my mother's mother began to verbally attack my father for some minor grievance because, well, she was the matriarch and perhaps felt it her right. It was back in the states, while she was visiting from the island. My father had walked her to the bus stop in Yonkers so she could catch the bus to the train station. And she began to nag. And nag. Relentlessly. Zealously. But he, keeping his mouth shut, waited patiently in silence with her until the bus arrived. When it arrived, she was so deep in her nagging that she was oblivious to the bus's arrival and, still steeped in her verbiage onslaught, the bus shut its doors without her and drove off. The second bus arrived with the same results. The third bus came and still she was so engrossed in her nagging spree that she ignored the bus and it left. The fourth bus arrived and, while she was still nagging, my father picked her up by the elbows and placed her on the bus, paid her fare and stepped back down as the bus door shut and began to drive off, my grandmother still nagging at him from inside the bus. It wasn't until the bus drove one block that my grandmother came out of her nagging stupor and realized that she had been verbally lacerating an advertisement for chewing gum posted against the bus wall.

The next day she returned to my father's house and, a bit sheepishly, knocked on the door. My father answered, saw her, and a broad smile washed over his face. He extended both his arms and pulled her in with a hug saying, "Vre kalostina:" one of the friendliest welcomes one could receive, full of warmth and belonging. She admitted that she had no idea how he would receive her, and, knowing her nagging was way out of line, was vastly relieved to have been so immediately and thoroughly forgiven. He never brought up the incident from the day before. Nor did she. And my father, mother and grandmother sat down to a feast of bean soup, greens and gossip from the island. And that, I learned, was the way to truly live – and to live deliberately.

Another factor to their longevity, is that they never cooked from pre-packaged, processed foods. Everything my parents and grandparents made came from scratch. Everything. And this is the way I cook. It's not much more trouble to make a good vegetable soup from scratch than it is to go to the store and buy the canned varieties. The homemade is always superior and has less sodium and unadvertised chemicals.

And then there are the arts; making the violins that make the music, weaving the rugs and blankets of wool, rugs and blankets that keep loved ones warm, rugs and blankets that have the feel of love in the touch of the fibers; exploring the flowers and knowing where the mushrooms are nestled under the pine needles; and swimming in the sea, keeping senses alert to catch any archeological finds. My father once found the marble head of a lion that had somehow washed ashore. Many years later it was still one of the highlights of his life. But so was his mother's love, her gentle philosophy that shaped his own – how she would never kill a hen who became too old to lay eggs, but instead allowed the hen to live out her life naturally until the end in appreciation of her service to the family.

But mostly, it was in the family that surrounded you; cousins, aunts and uncles who might not really be your cousins, aunts or uncles, but were honorary members of your family. It's knowing that while they could sometimes stifle you, they also had your back. You were never isolated or alone. They would never permit it because your life was too important to them. It is in the society of our family that we learn of the importance of our own lives. We have lost that in this country, except for such groups as the Amish. We have become islands unto ourselves, detached from the living fiber of each other. No Facebook account or Tweets could ever take the place of sitting among family and friends in a cafeneio, meeting glowing eyes that embrace you and receiving spiritual warmth from those who sit around the table with you, even if this is only just the first time you've met and even if it is outside under a chilly midnight sky.

The cold reality is that we are here for a finite period of time. It is good to learn to make our enjoyment of it infinite. When all is said and done, that is perhaps the wisest thing we could ever do.

Chapter Two

IKARIA, THE ISLAND: A PRIMER

Local folklore has it that after creating the earth, God found Himself with a pile of leftover rocks for which He no longer had any use. These He flung over His shoulders – and the island of Ikaria was born.

My family on the Lefas side, with a group of several other families, left their ancestral home of Sparta, Greece, in the 1600's, and migrated to the Aegean island of Ikaria in search of the vast pine forests, untouched wildernesses and promises they believed the deserted island proffered. In fact, the island had been inhabited since around 7000 BC, but continuous piracy raids frightened inhabitants to either leave the island, or hide inside its many crevasses, hand-hewn underground tunnels, natural caves and rock fortifications. There the newly arrived migrants settled among the rocks on which the mythological Icarus crashed with his melted wax wings after flying too close to the sun. And there, in the midst of Ottoman Empire rule, they began the arduous task of eking out a living from rock and sea. Learning to forage for readily available and nutritious greens was one way they were able to survive. Indeed, the age-old practice of foraging for wild greens is one of several factors that Dan Buettner, who included Ikaria in his Blue Zone where people live heartily until ripe old ages, noted. It is an art that has been passed on from parent to child. My grandmother was very adept at this and taught me well, and today, instead of spinach in my spanakopita, I will often make it with Vleeta, (amaranthus viridis, from the Goosefoot Family of plants), lamb's quarters mixed with fresh, young dandelion leaves or, on occasion, turnip leaves which have grown wild in the garden. No one notices the switch.

In ancient times, Ikaria, known locally as Nikaria, had other names such as Makris, Doliche and Ichthyosesa. Famous for its wine, Homer mentioned it in his Iliad and Odyssey. Plato, who learned much from his life-affirming mentor Socrates, mentioned Ikarian wine in his Republic of Plato, and many others sang its praises as well. To further create an indelible link between Ikaria and wine, the mythological god of wine, Dionysos was said to have been born in the ancient city of Drakanos, which is now part of Agios Kirykos, the present day capital of the island.

For nearly 400 years after the settlers arrived from Sparta in the 1600s, the isolated and harsh lifestyle of Ikarians hardly changed, yet, despite that, they flourished, cooked, ate and enjoyed life. Today, Ikaria is a robust social mecca and people come from as far away as Sweden, Denmark, Norway, Germany and the USA, and as nearby as the tiny island of Patmos (of the Book of Revelation / Apocalypse fame), to party. This is a prime example of the Ikarian heritage; the persistent reinvention of life. Despite hardships, and there were many, Ikarians honed the skill of familial strength, resourcefulness and defiant tenacity, with a healthy dose of humor. Ferociously independent, the centuries of working together, a necessity of survival, also created a devout sense of hospitality generously given to anyone who walks through their doors. My aunt calls it Φιλότιμος, (fil-O-tea-mos) which simply means being zealous of one's pride or honor, or having a worthy self-esteem. On the island one can easily translate this to one's sense of pride in providing hospitality to the sojourner.

When I stayed in Ikaria, I was immediately and eagerly swept into the large circle of family and friends whom I had never before met. There, walking down the main drag of Agios Kirykos was as much a family reunion – every single time – as it was a path on which I did my errands. Cousins owned shops and cafes, and homes were always open for impromptu visits. This is what I miss the most – the casual ambling about, dropping in an unsuspecting relative's home and being treated like a queen. But their hospitality and ease of life was not confined to wayward American relatives. Once, while sitting in a cousin's house, I saw a man walking up to my cousin's almond tree in the front garden and, in broad daylight, stripping it of almonds. I alerted my cousin to the casual theft and he just shrugged his shoulders carelessly with, "That's OK. I took two pounds of his olives yesterday." Life on the island is also about give and take.

To understand Greek food, particularly Ikarian food, one must understand the land from where it is cultivated. Ikaria, like most of Greece, is a land of two colors; the blue, cloudless sky reflecting radiantly off the bluer Aegean, and white buildings that glisten mutely under the blinding light of a white sun. And, like the rest of Greece, Ikaria is a stark mingling of old and new. One does not supersede the other, but merely accommodates the other. It is a land of new condominiums squatting against the backdrop of the ancient Tower of Drakano. The olive tree, fig tree and almond tree, anachronistic symbols, crowd private gardens of the ancient towns of Evdilos and Nas and spill over to the more modern port of Agios Kirykos.

The multi-faceted face of Ikaria may be taken for granted by its residents, but never the food, for food is an all-important factor; from solemn religious observances to every excuse for a party that has ever been conceived in the ambitious minds of men. Socrates once said, "Some men live to eat, but I eat to live." The Ikarians are loyal to Socrates' philosophy, to a point. But they are not unlike Anacreon, a poet of ancient Greece who lived to sing songs in praise of love and wine. The echo of his songs can still be heard resounding from the hearts of the blindly romantic, but even this has been tempered by the Ikarians. They have found a happy medium between Socrates's philosophy and Anacreon's passion as they focus their alert attention toward the realistic benefits of artistic cuisine.

The Greeks' association with food borders on a love affair. Perhaps it is because it reflects their enjoyment of life and their ingrained tradition of anabiosis; a restoration of life from death. Their ancient plays are full of it. Comedy, after all, was born of tragedy.

Though I had sampled some of the most exotic food Greece had to offer, the most memorable meal I have ever enjoyed in my parents' island was on the shores of Agios Kirykos. There, amidst chattering children and gossiping adults, I sat down to a chunk of white bread, a dish of sardines, a slab of feta cheese, a slice of tomato and a glass of red wine. It was simple fare, but the wind was Aegean soft like the rosy glow of the setting sun, the damp fragrance of wisteria wafted through the air like a lacy ribbon, and life was care-free. What made that meal special was not my hunger, nor the mysterious ingredients used in its preparation, but the full, robust life exploding and the interchange of love weaving around me. I ate that food with a love of that life and an appreciation of all things deep and beautiful, and was keenly mindful that every bite was a celebration of that love. In the slow pace of that warm Aegean evening, in the midst of the happy noise of the children and open heartedness of the adults, I learned the secret of anabiosis, I felt its power, and for that moment, I became just a little more human.

These recipes cannot recreate the awakening of one's awareness of life, for that is something every soul must discover on its own. These recipes, however, reflect some of the wonder of that celebration of life. Enjoy!

Chapter Three

THE CUISINE
Begins with Appetizers

When my father, a chef in Manhattan whose first inklings of cuisine blossomed in the small Ikarian village of Perdiki, would ask his American-born progeny if we would like almond and rice stuffed grape leaves soaked in wine sauce or braised octopus for dinner and we would reply, "Peanut butter and jelly sandwiches, please," he would throw up his hands in despair and proclaim, "You Americans don't know how to eat!"

He was right. We didn't. At least not according to his standards. But we did learn to eat cold, raw squid that my father had the blissful, yet naive hope of turning into a sumptuous meal the next day. What did we know? As small children, my two brothers and I would raid the refrigerator at 6 AM on Saturday mornings for a fistful of pink, rubbery squid plastered in jelly before parking our padded rear ends in front of the TV for our weekly dose of cartoons.

Though I eventually learned that raw squid was not quite the delicacy my father had in mind, I never did learn to eat like a Greek until many years later when I lived in Greece and was practically force-fed by eager aunts and my father's mother who swore with every small bite I took that I would die of hunger before the day was out. There, in Greece, among the wild poppies and olive groves, I learned the art of dining and the mystery of food and gleaned, from every willing aunt and cousin, the secrets of their cult.

And while the rest of the world has succumbed to fast food and pre-packaged, processed foods, self-sufficient islanders on Ikaria (partly by reason of their semi-isolation), have stayed true to their ancient custom of dining as they have for centuries. They grow and cook from scratch – almost everything. And they forage. And they enjoy every taste sensation with relish.

APPETIZERS

DOLMADES: Stuffed Grape Leaves

As the only girl in the family, the job of hunting down grape leaves for dolmades fell squarely on me. My father had a small vineyard from which to garner tender young leaves, and failing this, the fence around the property was abundant with wild grape leaves.

I have used fresh grape leaves for this recipe, for that is all we ever used. But you can get grape leaves in jars, floating in brine, if fresh young grape leaves cannot be had. Just be certain to rinse the brine from the leaves, soaking the leaves in bowls of fresh water repeatedly until the heavy brine is mostly removed. For my money, nothing beats fresh. It is far less expensive, too.

This recipe is what my father taught me. My grandmother and mother preferred lemon drenched dolmades, but my father preferred wine. Wine soaked dolmades (the alcohol burns off during the baking process), is an aromatic dish and much enjoyed. It makes a great accompaniment to fish or lamb (poor lamb), or stands proudly on its own.

DOLMADES: Stuffed grape leaves made with wine sauce (or lemon juice)

About 120-150 fresh young, tender grape leaves, prepared (or 2 / 10 oz. jars of grape leaves in brine)
1/2 cup of olive oil
1 cup of slivered almonds, toasted
1 onion, finely chopped
1 large zucchini, grated
2 medium carrots, grated
4 ripe tomatoes, chopped
3 cups of cooked rice, (from anywhere that has not grown cotton on the same land prior as the arsenic levels are high in this regional rice)
2 teaspoons of sea salt
1 teaspoon of freshly ground pepper
1 bunch of fresh parsley, finely chopped
1 tbsp sage
3 cups red wine (alternatively; juice of 3 lemons)
3 cloves garlic that has been put through the garlic press

BLANCHING THE FRESH GRAPE LEAVES

- If using fresh grape leaves, blanch leaves in a large gallon pot by bringing water to boil. Add 1 tsp. salt and juice of half a lemon to water.
- Shut off heat and place leaves in pot for about 2-5 minutes, depending how tender the leaves are and how quickly they blanch.
- Remove with slotted spoon and continue until all leaves are blanched. Placing the leaves in a metal colander, which is then placed in the water, also helps facilitate the process.

THE FILLING.

- In a large saucepan, heat 1/2 cup of olive oil and sauté the onion for about 2-3 minutes
- Add grated zucchini, and carrots, and cook over low heat until tender.
- Add chopped tomatoes and continue to cook for 5 minutes.
- Remove from the heat and set aside to cool for 15 minutes.
- Put in a bowl.
- Add mixture to cooked rice.

- Add parsley, sage, slivered almonds, 1 cup of wine or juice of one lemon, depending on how you are making this, remaining salt, and pepper
- Mix well with a spoon until blended.

FILLING LEAVES & ROLLING METHOD

Using a workspace, place leaves shiny down, one at a time, cutting off stems.

Place a heaping teaspoon of the prepared filling in the center of each leaf.

Fold leaf ends gently together, covering the filling, keeping both ends tucked inside the folds. Place seam down on baking pan.

WINE SAUCE

Cook red wine and grated garlic together over low heat until garlic fragrance is released. Pour over dolmades.

If making dolmades with lemon, pour the juice of one or two freshly squeezed lemons over all dolmades at this point.

Cover dolmades pan with aluminum foil and bake at 350 for 30 minutes or until done.

Uncover pan, and let sit in hot oven an additional five minutes.

Serve hot.

Serve as an appetizer or as a main dish accompanied by crisp endive salad, cheese or Fresh Yogurt Cheese, and followed by Greek coffee.

SPANAKOPITA
Or Cheese and Spinach Pie

This is my favorite, a dish my mother taught me, who had learned it from her mother, who had learned it from her mother in the days when cooks made their own phyllo on the kitchen table; because after milking the goats and making yogurt and cheese, carding, washing and spinning sheep and goat's hair into yarn, weaving the rugs and blankets, crocheting sweaters, planting the garden, harvesting, drying and storing food in those pre-refrigeration days, foraging for wood for the hearth, making soap, making wine, making the pithos to hold the wine and digging into the earth to store it - they had nothing else to do but pound out wheat kernels on the old stone hand mill, make dough and spread it thin on the table over, and over, and over again, until the phyllo sheets were just right. These were the REAL Housewives.

SPANAKOPITA version 1

2 large onions, minced
1 clove garlic, minced
1 lb butter (four sticks) OR 2 cups olive oil, island style
3 (10 oz.) packages of frozen spinach
OR 4 cups fresh spinach
OR 4 cups fresh Vleeta
OR 4 cups fresh tender turnip leaves
6 eggs
1 lb. cottage cheese (I imagine the cottage cheese was a version of 'farmer' goat cheese)
½ lb. feta cheese, crumbled
OR 1lb Monterey jack or cheddar cheese, grated
½ cup parsley, mined
1 lb. phyllo pastry dough (found at local supermarket)
- Sauté onions and garlic in ¼ lb of butter (1/2 cup olive oil) till tender
- Cook spinach (or other greens) and drain, squeezing out excess water.
- Let cool

- In a large bowl, beat eggs till blended.
- Add cheeses, sautéed onion, garlic and minced parsley to mixture. Stir thoroughly.
- Butter a casserole dish or large baking pan.
- Place one sheet of phyllo in pan and brush with melted butter or olive oil with pastry brush.
- Continue till half the phyllo is used.
- Pour spinach and cheese mixture onto phyllo in pan and spread evenly, making sure to get the corners and sides so no one feels cheated when biting into end pieces.
- Top with remaining phyllo, brushing each sheet of phyllo with butter or oil as it is layered.
- Score top sheets with sharp knife into squares or diamonds.
- Bake at 325 degrees till top layer of phyllo is golden brown and cheese is melted.

Serves best warm. A real Mediterranean "comfort food."

SPANAKOPITA version 2

1 bunch minced scallions
1 large onion, minced
1 lb. butter
3 – 10 oz. pkgs. Frozen chopped spinach, two

packages fresh spinach
6 eggs
1 lb. cottage cheese
1 lb. feta cheese, crumbled or, if feta is out of reach, ricotta cheese will do.
Salt and pepper
1 lb. packaged phyllo

- Sauté onions and scallions in butter till tender.
- Cook spinach and drain thoroughly, squeezing out excess water. Cool.
- Beat eggs.
- Add cottage and feta cheese and mix well.
- Add onion mix and spinach.
- Season.
- In small pain melt remaining butter.
- Butter a large baking pan.
- Place one sheet of phyllo in the pan and brush with melted butter.
- Continue till one half of the phyllo is used.
- Spread spinach mixture over phyllo.
- Top with remaining sheets of phyllo, again brushing each sheet with butter.
- Score and bake at 325 degrees for 45 min. till golden and done.

Some Ikarian versions use only olive oil and skip the step of layering and coating each phyllo sheet with olive oil. Instead they pour olive oil on top of the completed Spanakopita before baking.

SQUASH CAKES

1 -1 ½ pounds zucchini or other summer squash
1 cup cracked meal flour
3 tbsp. grated cheese
1 onion, diced
2 eggs
Parsley, salt and pepper to taste

- Peel zucchini. Grate with coarse grater.
- Salt and let stand about half an hour
- Squeeze out water.
- Mix with parsley, cracked meal, cheese, eggs and onions.
- Take one spoonful of mixture and roll in flour, then shape into flat, round cakes.
- Fry in olive oil on low flame until golden brown.

MUSHROOMS WITH WINE

1 lb. small sized mushrooms
½ cup olive oil
Juice of one lemon
½ lb. tomatoes
1 bay leaf

¼ cup red wine
½ tsp. dried or 1 tsp. fresh minced oregano
½ tsp. dried or 1 tsp. fresh minced rosemary
salt and pepper to taste

- In a skillet, pour olive oil, lemon juice, tomatoes, bay leaf and sauté till tender.
- Add mushrooms and wine and continue to sauté for 10 additional minutes or until mushrooms are tender.
- Season with salt and pepper to taste

Serve as a side dish on its own, accompanied with bread, or as a sauce over braised vegetables, dolmades or fish or meat..

EGGPLANT SPREAD

4 eggplants
Olive Oil
½ cup parsley, chopped
2 cloves garlic, minced
½ green pepper, minced
1 onion, minced
½ red sweet pepper, minced
½ green pepper, minced
3 scallions, minced
4-8 black olives, diced

½ cup olive oil
¼ cup wine vinegar
salt and pepper and rosemary to taste

- Wash eggplants and rub with oil, piercing skin with a fork.
- Bake at 400 degrees for 45 minutes till soft
- Cool, peel and chop into a paste
- Mix the rest of the ingredients until all are well incorporated. Place all in blender if desired to get a very creamy consistency.

This paste goes very well on crackers, bread or *Paxemadia* (dried bread).

TIROPITES (Cheese Pie) version 1

I practically lived on these when I lived in Greece. You could say I was addicted. We all have our weaknesses.

These are ideally made with goat cheese or all feta but, if that cannot be had, any cheese will do. I like putting mozzarella and cheddar together for this.

1 lb packaged phyllo (unless you are one of those brave souls who makes your own)
1/2 lb feta cheese, crumbled
8 ounces ricotta cheese or cottage cheese
4 ounces of cheddar, grated

4 ounces mozzarella, shredded
3 eggs
½ onion, diced (optional)
salt and pepper
1/2 lb butter, melted

- Blend cheeses and onion and mix thoroughly.
- Add eggs, one at a time, and mix well
- Butter baking pan
- Place phyllo on pan, sheet by sheet, brushing each sheet with butter before layering on the next.
- Continue until you have used up half a pound of phyllo
- Pour cheese mixture on phyllo
- Finish layering phyllo as before, brushing after each additional sheet.
- Score lightly with knife in squares or triangle shapes.
- Bake at 350 degrees till phyllo is golden brown and cheese bubbles.
- Let cool
- Continue cutting through the previous scoring.
- Cover with the remaining half pound of phyllo, brushing each layer with butter.
- Bake at 350 degrees for 15 - 18 minutes, until golden brown. Serve hot.

OR – you can simply layer out half the package of phyllo, pour on the cheese and egg mixture and cover with remaining phyllo then pour olive oil atop all and bake. This gives a decidedly different taste, but it is also more in line with Ikarian cooking, as butter was traditionally scarcer than olive oil.

CHEESE FILLED PASTRY version 2

½ lb. feta cheese, crumbled
½ lb cottage cheese
½ lb butter, melted
1 lb. phyllo
3 eggs

- Blend crumbled feta and cottage cheese and mix thoroughly.
- Add eggs, one at a time, and mix well
- Butter baking pan
- Place phyllo on pan, sheet by sheet, brushing each sheet with butter before layering on the next.
- Continue until you have used up half a pound of phyllo
- Pour cheese mixture on phyllo
- Finish layering phyllo as before, brushing after each additional sheet.

- Score lightly with knife in squares or triangle shapes.
- Bake at 350 degrees till phyllo is golden brown and cheese bubbles.
- Let cool
- Continue cutting through the previous scoring.

Serve as an appetizer or as a main dish accompanied by crisp endive salad, cheese or Fresh Yogurt Cheese, and followed by Greek coffee.

Chapter Four

WHAT GOES BEST WITH CHEESE PIE, BUT GREEK COFFEE?

Coffee was very important to my grandmother. Not only did it provide a restorative kick, but it was useful in telling the future. And for telling the future, nothing did the trick better than the muddy grounds of Greek Coffee. Her own daughter, my mother, did not suffer this nonsense quietly, but in me, my grandmother had found new hope.

Superstition was not really a requirement in old-school Ikaria – but it was useful, and entertaining, and learning to be able to tell the future by the way the thick grounds of Greek coffee coated the inside of the cup could, depending upon your ability, give you a sort of rock star prominence among the old grandmothers of the island. It was unreliable and unnecessary, but it was intriguing and somehow, comforting. My grandmother would take her cup after draining the last bit of muddy coffee and, like a scientist fixated upon the lab results of a test tube, tilt the cup forward and back, swirl it around, then analyze the grounds.

"Ah," she would exclaim at last. "You see how the grounds fall? It means your grandfather, he comes into money." She was very pleased with her deduction.

I thought the grounds fell the way they did because of a thing called gravity, but I was smart enough not to breathe a word of this to her. Satisfied that the muses had spoken to her via spent ground beans, she then shifted her focus from the cup to me and thrust the cup into my hands.

"Here, you try," she commanded.

I grabbed the coffee cup and looked back at her with the dumb look of the unenlightened. "What do you want me to try?" Oh, the bliss of ignorance!

She sharpened her blue eyes on me so swiftly that if I were a food item, I would have already been diced and sliced and thrown into the pot. But I was not a food item. I was her granddaughter – injudicious, unperceptive and downright obtuse. But I had good qualities, too. I could be taught. There went that blind faith.

"You," she said patiently, sweetly, slowly, trying to control her exasperation, "try to read the coffee grounds. What do you see?"

I looked at the cup that by now had morphed into a beleaguered, almost human like entity that had hoped my discernment of its special properties would rescue it from the shelf of the damned and give it a reason to go on being a cup. But all I could only see was the obvious.

"Coffee grounds," I was honest. And it was dangerous.

My grandmother shook her head in defiance of the truth – that her granddaughter was a hopeless ignoramus.

"No. Tell me what you really see. The grounds, they fall a certain way and they speak to you. What do they look like? Use your imagination."

"Oh, so imagination is what fortunetellers use? In that case, I could be really good at this."

Again, those swift, incisive, razor sharp eyes. No words were necessary. I focused. I squeezed my imagination, drop by stingy drop onto the forefront of my mind.

The coffee grounds, by reason of their being batted about a bit by an impatient soothsayer – my grandmother – did look a bit like a blotchy waterfall. And this was the answer I delivered to my grandmother.

"A waterfall???!!!" She drew in a sharp breath and calmed herself. She drew in another sharp breath. Patience. Patience was important. Patience could teach even a mule a few lessons.

"Try it again," she said at length in a low, measured tone.

I held up the cup and twisted it this way and that. The only thing I could truly see was a cup in desperate need of a wash. There were no magical messages in it. There was no good fortune coming down the pike either, unless, of course, it arrived in the form of a soapy sponge.

Rattled with naked impatience now, she snatched the cup from my hand and held it up discerningly.

"Yes," she nodded her head sagely, trying to redeem my insouciance. "Yes. You grandpapa, he come into money."

"Yes, he will," I agreed. "He owns a restaurant. He comes into money every day."

Practicality had no place in my grandmother's arsenal of perdition.

"Prediction," she corrected.

GREEK COFFEE

Greek coffee is like regular coffee... actually no, it isn't. It's espresso mixed with rocket fuel. It's coffee you might actually try to eat with a fork. It is boiled thrice, watched over and protected. It is only made in small quantities. If made well enough, you can use it for barter at the World Bank – or even use it as a corner stone for the World Bank. It is not for the faint of heart. The grounds are never quite fully separated from the rest of the coffee and you must be prepared to chew your coffee as much as drink it. You have to allow most of the grounds to settle gingerly on the bottom of the cup on their own time – not yours. That may be one reason why the Ikarians are notoriously late for any appointment – for they have to wait for the grounds to settle first, (that, and they religiously ignore clocks).

An Englishman (true story) got off the boat at Agios Kirykos and inquired about a bus to get from that port town to nearby Therma where the hot springs are.

"Is there a bus here?" he asked one shopkeeper.

The shopkeeper said, yes, there was a bus.

"Where would I wait for it?" the Englishman asked next.

"Right here by the corner," the shopkeeper said.

"When will the bus come?'

"It will come. It will come." The shopkeeper assured him.

And so the Englishman dutifully waited at the corner. For hours. Finally, by nightfall, the weary Englishman asked the shopkeeper, "When WILL the bus driver be here?"

"When he wakes up," was the reply.

I blame it on Greek coffee.

The Coffee

Though you really, seriously and in all honesty cannot tell the future by the way the grounds coat the inside of the cup, Greek coffee, once called Turkish coffee, is still one of the nicest things the Ottoman Empire left us. It is a rich coffee that diversifies easily with spices, and the aroma of this strong, potent nectar is always enjoyed amidst the company of friends and family. Just the fragrance alone evokes close familial ties. They can keep big box store coffees. This is the real deal.

You will need a special brewing pot called an ibrik and readily available online. It is shaped like a mini pot with a narrow neck and spout, and a long handle. It holds one or two servings, sometimes more. This is the specialty of Greek Coffee. It is said that the pot was shaped that way to get optimal benefit from absorbing the heat from the hot sands in the deserts of the Mideast on which food, and coffee, were cooked and brewed. Today the stove top works wonders.

So – you will need:

1 ibrik – 4 oz. You could go for an 8 oz or a 12 oz, but for the purpose of this recipe, I will be using 4 oz.

Two heaping tsps of Greek coffee – finely ground like powder

Sugar to taste (one tbsp for me, but common usage is around 2 tsps.)

Enough water to fill the ibrik up to the first narrowing of the neck. Now comes the art.

- First is the sugar. You place sugar in the empty ibrik.
- Fill the ibrik with water to the point where the neck narrows. Stop it there, as you will need the extra space for the resulting foam later.
- Place two heaping teaspoons of Greek Coffee in the pot. The coffee grounds will

float on the water. Resist the temptation to stir. They are supposed to float. There's a science to that, but you will have to ask someone else.

- Place the ibrik on your stove and heat it slowly. Medium heat works, too. Resist the temptation to ignore it to check your twitter. It will boil quickly and an unattended ibrik is a fearsome thing to experience.
- The water is supposed to develop a foam on the neck. If it boils instead, you did not use enough coffee. Simmer until foam develops. As the foam begins to grow up the neck of the ibrik, watch it. As soon as the foam threatens to overflow, take it off its heat source and gingerly stir the foam until it is settled.
- Repeat this step twice. On the third time, allow the foam to swell up the neck of the pot, but do not stir. Remove it from its heat source.
- Gently scoop up the foam and place it in your cup. Or, if you do not like the foam, discard it.
- Allow the coffee grounds to settle for about 30 seconds, then pour your coffee. You may top it off with cream. The bottom of

the ibrik will resemble mud after all the coffee is enjoyed. Resist the temptation to tilt it to read your fortune. The boiled grounds all look like waterfalls, anyway.

- For a real Moroccan delight, add ½ tsp. cinnamon, ¼ tsp. ginger and 1/8 tsp pepper to each 4 oz. of coffee before brewing.

Chapter Five

HOWEVER . . .
FIRST THINGS FIRST: SWEETS
(Preserves)

There are certain things a Greek girl is supposed to know beyond a shadow of a doubt, and one of them is that if you leave lint on the silverware because you've forgotten to starch your linen towel, you will surely never catch a husband. The other is that a way to a man's heart is through his stomach, and male stomachs preferred dolmades to hamburger and a good square of baklava to chocolate cake. It was not at all true, but I, born in Brooklyn and very much part of the American culture, did not have the heart to tell my grandmother.

My mother's mother, whom I called Yiayia, was determined that an American upbringing would not hinder all the life-truths a proud and faithful Greek matriarch was indicted to pass on to her female progeny. I was daily briefed on proper scrubbing habits for window corners and garage ceilings, the proper way to starch, and iron, a linen dish towel (!), how to fold that dish towel using the tread marks of a hot iron to steam the edges into a crisp, clean line, how to iron freshly laundered bed sheets, and pressed into the service of washing china plates until the reflection of my face revealed every pore and hair follicle. She took great pains in teaching me many other useless things that men, Greek or American, could care less about. I was a poor student. The writing was on the wall. I would never marry and die an old maid. It was enough to send my grandmother into fits of focused religious observance and many prayers were uttered to the heavens on my behalf. Nothing was more shameful than a Greek woman who never married.

No one worked harder than my Yiayia, whose perfect aquiline nose and high cheek- bones would have, in another culture, assured her a life of leisure and wealth instead of labor. I had been told by many aunts while sitting under the grape arbor of my great-aunt's house, that my grandmother was the most beautiful of all the girls from the island of Ikaria. When she was sixteen-years-old, her long white-blond hair was the talk of all the villages, and her ice blue eyes the envy of all the swarthy girls. The day she married, the entire village turned out and lined the streets to see her beauty. My grandfather, just seventeen and impetuous, married the woman he would love for the next sixty-two years, though it cost him a spanking by his own father the day after the wedding. By the time I knew my Yiayia, her long, flowing hair had turned silver and was kept in a tight bun, but her blue eyes were incisive like scalpels; beautiful to look at if she was not cross with you and fiery portals of righteous indignation if she was. Her beauty still caught the breath of the men of her generation. She was sharp like a razor when it came to business matters and worked by the side of my grandfather in every restaurant they ever owned. They bought a house in Bayport, Long Island, after spending the earlier part of their American lives in a Brooklyn brownstone, and immediately painted it white with sea-blue shutters because they had grown homesick for their white marble and blue island. Their house was only about twenty steps from the Great

South Bay and was their reward after a hard day's work.

Yiayia taught me to read Greek before I could read English, and she scolded me in Greek before I could sass back in English. She was the only woman I ever knew who could look crisp and clean, even in the middle of the summer over a steaming pot of boiling water. Her light blue dresses were starched and bright and she never ventured out of her bedroom in the morning until she looked like she had just stepped out of a fashion catalogue. Neat to a fault, clean to an obsession, she expected the very same of me. But I was my father's daughter, not my mother's.

One day my Yiayia and Papou (my grandfather), along with my uncle and parents, headed out in search of a solitary aunt. This tenacious aunt had deftly managed her own domicile and garden, even after the recent loss of her husband. Her house was typical of the island's older homes; built of rock with a rock slab roof and blue painted shutters on narrow windows. It squatted firmly into the side of the rock from whence it seemed hewn. On the way to her front door was a white trellis arbor laden with thick purple grapes. Tomatoes lined her walkway and vivid flowers wove a ballet across the outside walls. Anyone else might have let that small postage stamp-sized piece of real estate become a dust bin, but the islanders know how to make a limited space work wonders and every nook and cranny of that postage stamp choked with wonder. Bright magenta roses with raspberries and cucumbers grew up the sides of the fence. Cherry, lemon and orange trees flanked the sides of the house like faithful sentinels. Instead of rambling grass there was a manicured vegetable garden deftly calculated to maximum potential. Inside the small structure, after you passed the gauntlet of vegetation, was my aunt's kitchen with bean stew bubbling on an old wood stove in a secluded corner. Dark swags of crimson material doubled for doors, and icons of the Madonna and Christ Child blessed the humble dwelling with their somber gaze and entreating gestures. A candle burned for the dead, in this case her husband, and I was scolded for washing the dishes we had used for she had no one to speak to after we left, and cleaning the dishes gave her something to do.

She was short, like her countrymen, and shorter yet because of her age. She was not pristinely dressed like my Yiayia, and Yiayia seemed to compassionately forgive her for this. Needles and safety pins stuck out of her worn house-dress, and her hair was a wiry jungle of gray. Her eyes were sad ones, with dark circles weighing down any facial animation, but she was soft-spoken and eager to exchange island gossip. She gave us a spoon of cherries in a thick sweet syrup called 'glyco' that was eaten slowly by dipping the cherry syrup laden spoon in a glass of water and then sucking on it. It is an old Greek recipe from the island, and Yiayia pointed it out like a professor would a good book in a library, "You will learn to make this koukla-mou (my doll), because you will be able to catch a husband this way."

"So, you have a boyfriend?" my aunt became animated.

"She is just a young girl," Yiayia corrected politely. "But she is learning to cook and clean and should have no trouble finding a husband."

"Yes," the aunt agreed politely, "No man wants a girl who does not know how to cook and clean. He will want to know if your Yiayia has taught you this. So, if you want to marry, you must cook and clean everything."

"Why don't the men cook and clean, too," I asked, because the men of our small party had taken themselves out to the garden to sit under the grape arbor while the stew was cooking and I was pressed into service to trim the green beans and separate the Vleeta leaves from the bugs and grit.

"Men work outside, women work in," Yiayia could be very logical, but her argument was weak.

"But you work outside the home with Papou in the restaurant and you work inside, too, doing all the women's work. Why doesn't Papou help you cook and clean inside the house as well?"

"Achoo!" the aunt exclaimed and, looking at the Blessed Virgin, made the sign of the cross to atone for my ignorance. "Because a man's home is his castle. That is why. And it is the woman who must keep it that way. Why do you think he marries her anyway?"

"To be his free maid? Doesn't he have to love her?" I asked, stepping my ignorance up to sedition.

"Achoo!" she exclaimed again and glanced apologetically at Madonna, then threw the ball in my grandmother's court. "She is your granddaughter. You speak to her!"

Yiayia's blue eyes darkened with the task of remonstration as they fell squarely on me. Not only was I never going to get married, I was going to burn in hell, too, for no Madonna could put up with the foolishness I was displaying. She stared at me for a long while, trying to figure out the puzzle that was her progeny. Surely there had been a mistake when ordering granddaughters. And then, I watched her face as illumination edged out despair.

"She is an American," Yiayia explained at length with relief while still looking at me. "She does not know better."

"Ah," the aunt nodded with sudden understanding. And instantly, I was relegated to those hapless and unfortunate souls who had the misfortune of not being born in the 'old country,' though that was the direct result of my grandparents' and father's pioneering ambitions. Yiayia did not bother her head with the details.

"You will marry a nice Greek boy from Ikaria," Yiayia proceeded to lay down the law, "He will be a good husband to you, and you will cook and clean for him."

"But I want to be a nurse."

"You can nurse your husband and children when they are sick. Men, they should go to school. You, you should learn to be a good Greek girl and learn to make glyco."

"The men, they like to talk," the aunt explained. "Talk, talk, talk. Always the talk! But, that is what they do. And they like to eat. So, we let them talk and we make them food. This way, they will be comfortable. And a comfortable man never strays."

I glanced outside to the garden where my father, grandfather and uncle were knee deep in light banter. I had not thought of men as strays. Dogs, yes, but never men. My father never strayed. And, as a chef, he cooked! So did Papou in his own restaurant. I wondered who wrote the rulebook and if it was still in print. Probably some wise soul tossed it overboard on the way to the new world. But they were certain to rip the recipes from the book first – and this is why I still have them.

GLYKO (γλύκο) - SWEETS

Traditional glyko offers aesthetic beauty, which feeds the soul, and palatial legitimacy which feeds the stomach.

The proper way for guests to enjoy the jam is to dip the fruit or rose jam laden spoon into the glass, then nibble a taste, followed by a sip of water.

ROSE PETAL JAM

(My favorite. I like to make huge batches every summer. The yield makes great gourmet gifts for the following Christmas, and because the jam retains the fragrance of the roses, it's like eating a spoonful of summer sun in the dead of winter. And no, this did not land me a husband. Sorry, Yiayia.)

4 cups pesticide, fungicide free rose petals (fragrant tea roses are best)
4 cups sugar
4 cups water or enough to cover the petal/sugar mixture (can be augmented with rose water found in ethnic specialty shops)
2 tsp. lemon juice (to preserve color)
¼ tsp. cream of tartar (optional)

- Prepare roses by cutting whole heads of fresh, lively roses (I choose those hidden out of view so as not to spoil the display) and place in a large mixing bowl.
- Carefully, grab a single rose head at a time, grasping tightly onto the outer edges of petals. Holding firm, pull petals from core and snip off white ends with scissors (white ends can give a bitter taste to the jam). Toss white ends back into the garden. Place the rest of the petals in a mixing bowl.

- Cover petals with sugar. Set aside overnight, tossing occasionally with fork to incorporate.
- Bring water to a boil in a large, heavy pot. Add sugared petals and remaining ingredients, stirring gently until sugar melts.
- Reduce heat and simmer for 45 minutes until jam thickens. It should reach 220 degrees on candy thermometer, but I usually just go by sight and test – if a drop of jam gently solidifies in a cup of cold water, it is done.
- Cover pot the last ten minutes of cooking time to wash down the sugar crystals on sides of pot. When cooled, pour into clean, sterilized jars. Seal tightly with lids. I like to can them in a boiling bath for extra measure. Small jelly jars are best. These keep very well.

 * A note: Honeysuckle flowers or any aromatic flower, may be substituted for roses

CHERRY SPOON PRESERVES
3 pounds of fresh cherries (slightly under ripe)
6 1/2 cups of white sugar
1 tsp fresh lemon juice (to preserve color)

- Pick cherries when they are ripe and firm
- Wash the cherries well.
- Remove stems and pits without damaging the fruit, and place in colander over sink to drain.
- Combine water and sugar in a pot and bring to a boil over medium heat, stirring gently.
- When syrup thickens to the consistency of maple syrup, remove from heat and allow to cool.
- Add cherries to the syrup and bring to a hard boil.
- Skim off foam as it rises to the surface.
- Add the lemon juice.
- Bring to boil again for about another minute and immediately remove from heat. Store in small canning jars made for jam and preserves.
- Process for 10 minutes to keep preserves from spoiling or store in airtight containers in the refrigerator.

GRAPEFRUIT PRESERVES
6 grapefruit
3 lbs. sugar
3 cups water

2 tbsp. Lemon juice

- Grate rind of fruit down till you hit the white inside of rind
- Section while grapefruit lengthwise into 8 slices each.
- Remove fruit from rind entirely.
- Roll up each section of rind and thread through with darning needle and heavy thread.
- Tie ends to prevent unrolling or hold in place with toothpick
- Place strings of rolled grapefruit rind in large pot of water rand boil for 30 minutes till tender.
- Drain
- Boil again but only till water boils.
- Drain and repeat in fresh water.
- Drain and leave in fresh water overnight. This should clear most of the bitterness of the rind.
- The next day drain and place strings on clean, dry towel to absorb moisture.
- To make thick syrup: Boil sugar, water and lemon juice together.
- Test. When syrup is a medium, ball stage, it is ready

- Carefully remove string from rind rolls and place fruit in syrup.
- Simmer for 5 minutes, remove from heat and let stand for 12 hours.
- The following day, boil fruit again until syrup is thick.
- Pack in sterile jars and preserve.

.

FIG PRESERVES
2 lbs figs, unpeeled
3 cups granulated sugar
1 cup water
1/2 cup of freshly squeezed lemon juice

- Prepare figs by gently washing each one, careful not to bruise the skin, and cut off all stems and blemishes. Cut figs in half.
- Completely cover figs with water in a large pot and soak for at least half an hour.
- Meanwhile, combine sugar, water and lemon juice and boil for about 10 minutes or until thickened to the consistency of maple syrup.
- Add figs and bring to a rolling boil. Boil hard for one minute, then reduce heat and simmer, stirring gently for about 20

- minutes, or until figs are quite tender and the liquid has evaporated by one third.
- Remove from heat. Seal in sterilized canning jars in halves, or mash first with a

- potato masher, or pulse in blender, if you want more of a jam-like appearance.
- Can for 20 minutes. May also be frozen.

STUFFED FIGS

1 lb. dried whole figs
1 cup orange juice
1 tbsp lemon juice
1 ½ tbsp lemon peel
3 tbsp. sugar
1 Cup pecans or almonds
½ cup sugar

- Remove stem end from dried figs
- Combine orange juice, lemon juice and peel and 3 tablespoons of sugar.
- Pour over figs and heat mixture to boiling point.
- Simmer in covered saucepan until fruit is tender.
- Drain well
- Cool.

- Insert knife in stem end of fig and fill pocket with pecan or almond.
- Close opening and roll figs in one-half cup sugar.
- Let dry overnight before storing.

SESAME CANDY

1 lb sugar
4 oz. honey
½ cup water
½ lb. sesame seed

- Blend sugar and honey in pan.
- Add water and cook over low heat, stirring frequently about 12 minutes or to a soft ball stage (test by dropping a ball of the syrup in cold water and testing level of firmness).
- Remove and add sesame seed.
- Spread on buttered pan to ¾ inch thickness.
- When cool, cut into 2 x 1 inch pieces.

Chapter Six

FISH

While Ikarians eat fish and occasionally meat, their mainstay of food mainly consists of vegetables. Still, fish is a treat to be savored, often on a weekly basis. Fish has also lent itself to expose the cunning nature of man.

My father's father was fond of a certain type of fish. As they ate fish reservedly, a feast of fish was a festive event. And because hospitality was part of their social obligation, they were forbidden by civility to turn anyone away who came to their door at supper time. All food must always be shared with whoever comes to your door while you are eating, without reservation.

There was a man who lived on the island and, for whatever reason, was loathe to cook for himself. Or perhaps he simply enjoyed his meal with friends and family. Any friend or family member would do. It is also possible that, simply put, he was a freeloader.

He must have been very fit, for he combed the island's punishing mountain landscape every night, visiting one family and the next night, another, planning his visits exactly at suppertime. Knowing that perspective hosts could not, in all that was refined and cultured, turn him away, he made himself comfortable at other people's expense. The host was obliged to open his hearth to this man, and feed him. To do otherwise was simply the mark of an inhospitable savage. Ikarians were, and still are, governed by strong personal pride.

It was while sitting down to supper to eat this much anticipated fish, that the dreaded knock on the door occurred. Knowing this man's 'visiting' cycle had curved its way back to them, my grandfather told my grandmother to quickly hide the fish. She did so and, instead, brought out a plate of bread, some greens, and a bottle of wine. The man was welcomed inside my grandparents' hearth, sat down, and my grandmother laid out his plate for him. She served the bread and greens. He ate wholeheartedly and they, not so much. They gave him wine. They gave him more bread, more greens and more wine. And more bread. Finally, he rubbed his stomach. It was entirely too full.

"More bread or greens?" my grandfather asked.

"Oh no, thank you. I couldn't fit anything more in my stomach."

"Are you sure?" my grandfather asked guardedly.

"Absolutely."

"Positive?"

"Very."

"Eleni," my grandfather called out to my grandmother, "bring out the fish."

And my grandparents, with their fish all to themselves, ate in peace. I never learned if their visitor ever came round again at suppertime.

BAKED FISH WITH ONIONS, TOMATOES AND HERBS

2 lbs of the fresh caught fish of the day.

Juice of 1 lemon (or more, depending on your love of lemon juice)

3 large onions chopped.

3 garlic cloves, slivered.

2 or 3 good sized fresh tomatoes, skins, seeds and all (skins and seeds have holistic

properties)
Sea salt and pepper to taste
½ cup of fresh chopped chives
½ cup of fresh, chopped parsley
½ cup fresh, chopped basil
3 tbsps Olive oil.
½ cup red wine.
2 leaves of dried, crumbled nasturtiums –
optional
1 tbsp chopped, fresh mint leaves - optional
A dash of sugar to level the acid of the
tomatoes, if desired.

- Oil pan with olive oil.
- De-scale the fish, cut off head and fins and slice in half lengthwise. (cutting off the head and tail is my preference. Many opt to keep these bit of anatomy intact). Clean it out, leaving the white flesh intact. De-bone, careful to gently pull out the spine and all tiny bones. Rinse and pat dry.
- Lay fish in pan and pour on the lemon juice. Some people like to saturate their fish in lemon juice. This depends upon how many fresh lemons you have at your disposal, and your taste. I also like to slice the garlic and dot some of the tiny bits of the slices all over the fish.

- In a large frying pan, place enough olive oil to give a good coating. Place onions, garlic, chives, parsley, basil, sea salt and optional
- nasturtiums and mint leaves, and sauté till tender. Add tomatoes, wine and optional sugar.
- Stir over low heat until sauce cooks down and thickens slightly.
- Pour over fish and bake at 350 for about 30 minutes or until fish flesh flakes easily. Baste throughout the cooking process for a tender but not overcooked fish.

"ISLAND SIMPLE" COOKING

My mother's parents had left Ikaria and settled in Brooklyn, New York, and eventually ended up owning their own restaurant in Sayville, Long Island, NY, and, later, Glendale, California. While their menu was ripe with convoluted, elaborately prepared seafood platters, their own preference for cooking fish remained true to their island upbringing – simple, unpretentious and honest.

Though my grandparents had their business in Sayville, they made their home in Bayport, and this is where my brothers and cousins spent our young summers and really became entrenched in Ikarian gastronomy.

My grandmother used to take the fish in its entirety, de-scale it, and cut out all the insides via what amounts to a C-Section. Then she would place the fish in the frying pan, tail, head, fins and all, and fry it up in olive oil and lemon. And then, much to my childish horror, she would lovingly place the fish which, to my eyes, seemed to be at least as long as the George Washington Bridge, on a plate with a side of olives and fresh picked greens, and assault me with the dreaded command bursting through pretty rosebud lips – "Eat!" The juxtaposition of the rosy lips and the words that sawed their way out of them was incongruous to everything Mother Goose taught me. Dr. Seuss, more like.

I looked at it and I looked at her, and she smiled sweetly at me, pleased that she was doing her bit to keep body and soul together. But what she grew up loving, I balked at. My spoiled American appetite would have preferred hot dogs or pizza. But instead, I had the carcass of an entire specimen of an alien marine life form laying on my plate, its bulging eyes boring reproachfully into mine, its mouth agape with teeth visible and threatening; and, I naturally assumed, still possessed with a bit of pulsating brain and a memory that would never, ever forget – or forgive. I had already planned to arm my room that night with my collection of dolls to stand as sentries around my bed. Oh, it made such perfect sense.

After she placed the plate in front of me, satisfied that she had given me ample to eat, she turned her attention toward other kitchen duties. Peaches were ripe on her trees out in the garden, and she was setting about to preserve at least half of them, while the other half of the harvest was reserved for fresh eating.

I watched her and, as any reasonable child would, began to plot. I shoved as much of the entire fish, head, tail and all, into my mouth as I could, and inaudibly announced that I had to run to the bathroom. There I released the contents into the toilet, flushed it, rinsed my mouth and returned brightly to the table. I repeated my actions. Rinse. Repeat. Rinse. Repeat. And like a minor miracle, the offending, albeit late, oceanic denizen was soon entirely purged from my plate. I was pleased with the inarguable fact that I was positively brilliant. With a tinge of smugness, I returned to my seat for what I thought would be the last time before play.

"I'm finished," I announced triumphantly at last to my grandmother whose wisdom had already run circles around me.

"Wonderful," she said with that firm smile. "But since you were so hungry that you ate the whole fish so quickly, here's more," and in one deft motion she lay another fish, intact, on my plate. It was obvious to me that she had been lying in wait for just this moment and calculated her timing like a Swiss watch. "And do NOT get up until you have finished your entire meal."

My parents had a more labor-intensive way of preparing fish, and it usually fell on me to carry out the labor. But if one was to eat fish, then surely one must take the time to make it less daunting to little children (just my world-view, not a universal truth). This simple island recipe, the way I remember my grandmother making it, served with the wild greens, sliced onions, lemon wedges and wine, could be a feast fit for a king.

SIMPLE IKARIAN FISH

1 whole fish of your preference, preferably the catch of the day.

½ cup Olive oil

1 lemon, sliced in thin slices. Keep the juice.

2 tbsp of fresh, chopped Chives or young wild onions, or 1 tbsp dried.
2 Onions. chopped
Sea salt and fresh ground pepper to taste.

- Descale the fish, remove head, tail and fins, and split open, careful to remove all the tiny bones.
- Rinse. Rub salt and pepper all over fish.
- Lay fish in roasting pan – or atop a frying pan on stove top.
- Pour olive oil, lemon slices, onions and chives, over the fish.
- Place in oven, if in a roasting pan, and place enough water to come up halfway the width of the fish. Or fire up the burner, if in a frying pan, which has been oiled with olive oil.
- Bake / Cook till tender and flakey and the aroma fills the house.

BAKED FISH AND VEGATABLE platter

1 large fish (bass, cod or whatever is fresh and immediately acquired).
1 cup olive oil
1 ½ cups of crushed or diced fresh tomatoes
1 cup white or red wine

Juice of half a lemon
3 onions, chopped
½ cup fresh parsley, chopped
2 cloves garlic, diced
Salt and pepper to taste.

Vegetables

1 lb fresh string beans
1 lb okra or squash blossoms, left whole or sliced
2 large potatoes, diced
2 medium zucchini squash, chopped
4 sticks celery, chopped
1 lb. fresh tomatoes, chopped, retaining health-benefit skins and seeds.
2 large onions, quartered and sliced
¼ cup chopped fresh dill or mint leaves
Salt and pepper to taste

- Clean and scale fish and wash thoroughly.
- Rub with salt and pepper and sprinkle with lemon juice.
- Fry onions and okra or squash blossoms in olive oil until golden brown.
- Add wine, tomatoes and seasoning
- Lay fish in greased (olive oil) baking pan and layer vegetables around it.

- Sprinkle with chopped parsley, dill or mint and garlic.
- Sprinkle olive oil on the vegetables.

- Add enough water to nearly cover the vegetables and bake, covered, at 350 degrees for about one hour
- Remove cover and continue baking until vegetables are tender and turn a gentle golden brown, and the flesh of the fish begins to flake.

EVEN MORE SIMPLE FRIED FISH

Though my father cooked complicated cuisine as a chef, at home he reverted back to his simple Island cooking which allowed the true flavor of the food to shine through.

This simple fish, with no bells or whistles but honest, good taste, goes well with rice with almonds and squash flowers, fresh Greek salad, clean cucumber slices, herb infused goat cheese and homemade red wine. It can also be served with a very basic dish of Vleeta (amaranthus viridis), a nutritional powerhouse that grows wild in the spring and summer across the globe, including both Greece and the United States of America. Like the nutritionally potent dandelion, it is considered a 'weed' by gardeners. Recipes for Vleeta follow.

FRIED COD IN BUTTER

1 cod fish, fresh or frozen, de-boned, skinned and sans head, fins or tail.

2 tbsps. Butter

Sea salt

- In a heavy frying pan, preferably a cast iron pan, melt butter over low flame.
- Place fish on pan and sprinkle lightly with sea salt.
- Fry on both sides till flesh flakes.

BOILED FISH WITH VEGETABLES

3 lb. fish

4 carrots

1 large onion

2 fresh tomatoes

3 potatoes

2 stalks celery

1 tbsp. chopped parsley

1 tbsp. lemon juice

3 tbsp olive oil

- Clean fish thoroughly and wipe with a damp cloth.

- Rub with salt and lemon juice and roll in flour.
- Tie in a piece of cheese cloth and put in saucepan.
- Cut all vegetables into small pieces and place in saucepan with fish.
- Pour three cups of boiling water with 3 tbsps. of olive oil and simmer for 30 minutes, or until fish is done.
- Remove fish and let cool
- Untie cheesecloth and remove fish to a larger platter.
- Carefully cut fish lengthwise in half, remove bones, and replace top half.
- Cover with mayonnaise and garnish platter with the boiled vegetables and black olives.
- Pour lemon sauce over all

STUFFED SQUID

12 squid
1 cup onions, chopped
2 tbsp parsley, chopped
½ cup olive oil
½ cup rice, boiled and strained
2 tbsps pignolias (pine nuts)
2 tbsps. tomato paste
2 tbsps chopped mint

salt and better
- Wash squid thoroughly, removing heads, bones and ink sacs.
- Cut the fins, leaving only the whole bag, and pulling out the black skin.
- Wash well and sprinkle with a little salt.
- Simmer onions and parsley and mind in sauce pan with olive oil until onion is golden brown.
- Add rice, pine nuts, tomato paste and salt and pepper to taste.
- Cook together a few minutes to blend flavors and set aside to cool
- Stuff each squid with a teaspoonful of above mixture and arrange side by side in baking pan.
- When all have been stuffed, pour on top sauce made of: 1 small glass wine, 3-4 tbsp olive oil, 3-4 tbsps. Water and salt and pepper.
- Bake at 350 degrees for about an hour.

Chapter Seven

SALADS

ON THE WILD SIDE

Salads are the quick picker-upper and, on the island, easily accessible. If your garden has not yet blossomed with lettuce, kale and endive, the hillsides most assuredly have. I've often thought Ikaria, with its abundant food grown in the wild as well as in its coddled gardens and with its long growing season, was as close to the Garden of Eden as any place on earth.

Sustainable, nutrition-packed free food under foot (just make sure they are pesticide-free and no animal has used them as a latrine. Wash very thoroughly)

VLEETA (Amaranthus viridis)

Vleeta is a great source of Vitamin A, C, and rich with minerals and other nutritional values.

DANDELION

Young dandelion leaves are an excellent source of antioxidants, high in iron, calcium, minerals and protein with all essential amino acids. Steam lightly or eat raw in salads.

CHICORY (as a green)

Like Vleeta and dandelion, chicory grows wild and abundant. While it has excellent medicinal properties, the leaves can be bitter. When using chicory as a side vegetable, boil chicory leaves in water and discard water. The second boil would eliminate further bitterness. Drain and sauté in garlic and olive oil, and season as desired. Makes a lovely, healthy dish when mixed with Vleeta and young, tender dandelion leaves. As my grandmother used to say, "It's good for the blood." Indeed.

LAMB'S QUARTERS

This is another wild, easily accessible 'weed' that is packed with nutrition which includes Niacin, Folate, Iron, Magnesium and Phosphorus, Protein, Vitamin A, Vitamin C, Thiamin, Riboflavin, Vitamin B6, Calcium, Potassium, Copper and Manganese. Is is also very low in Saturated Fat and Cholesterol. I used to confuse this with Vleeta because my grandmother called both Vleeta and Lamb's Quarters by the same name. Indeed, they closely resemble each other.

Great in fresh salads, sautéed with garlic, served with mushrooms or baby onions, dashed with the green tips of wild onions, this is very healthy repast.

These wild greens are an excellent, honest accompaniment to any fare, fresh, sautéed or steamed.

GREEK SALAD

1 romaine lettuce
2 cups endive
2 cups arugula
2 tomatoes, cut into wedges
4 green onions thinly sliced
9 black olives, halved and pitted

½ cup feta cheese, diced
- Mix all ingredients and toss with olive oil and vinegar, salt and pepper to taste

BEET SALAD

1 cup diced cooked beets
1 onion, minced
2 tbsps chopped fresh parsley
1 tbsp dill
olive oil
vinegar
salt and pepper to taste
- Combine all ingredients.
- Sprinkle liberally with oil and vinegar to taste.
- Chill and eat.

CHICORY SALAD

2 Romaine lettuce hearts
1 clove garlic
1 head young chicory
2 tbsps. minced onion
½ tsp. salt
¼ tsp. pepper
Feta cheese, optional
Tarragon vinegar

Olive oil

Rub salad bowl with clove of garlic.
Wash greens well.
Drain and chill until crisp
Line salad bowl with lettuce leaves.
Break chicory into large pieces.
Toss with just enough oil to coat salad greens
Add salt and pepper to taste
- Toss with vinegar and olive oil.
- Sprinkle crumbled feta cheese if desired.

SALAD BOWL WITH WINE VINEGAR

1 clove garlic
½ head lettuce
½ head escarole
½ head chicory (or tender dandelion leaves, lamb's quarters or vleeta if in season)
½ bunch watercress
¾ tsp. salt
Dash and pepper to taste
½ cup olive oil
4 tsps. Red wine vinegar
- Chop salad greens and mix together in bowl.

- Season with salt, pepper, olive oil and red wine vinegar and toss well.

EGGPLANT SALAD

4 small eggplants
3 tomatoes cut in eighths
2 tbsp. chopped parsley
1 tbsp
1 onion, diced
1 cup olive oil
3 tbsp wine vinegar
2 cups yogurt cheese (optional)
Salt and pepper to taste

- Bake the eggplants in a moderate oven till tender – about 1 hour.
- Remove, dip in cold water and peel.
- Dice eggplants and place in salad bowl.
- Add tomatoes, onion, parsley, olive oil, vinegar and season to taste.
- Stir well. Allow to marinate before serving.
- Top with yogurt cheese if desired

SUMMER SALAD

1 head lettuce
2 tomatoes, chopped
1 onion sliced in large rings

1 green pepper, seeded and chopped
1 cucumber, peeled, sliced
1 tbsp. chopped dill
½ tbsp rosemary
2 tbsps. almonds, slivered and toasted
½ cup olive oil
¼ cup wine vinegar
Seasoning to taste

- Mix all ingredients together and toss with wine vinegar and olive oil.

WILD BOUNTY ISLAND SALAD

Equal portions lamb's quarters, young dandelion leaves, vleeta, and tender turnip or beet greens to fill large salad bowl.

½ cup fresh chives, chopped
1 cup fresh, raw green beans, chopped in ½ inch pieces
1 cucumber, quartered and sliced thin
1 red onion, sliced in thin rings
2 tsps. chopped dill
1 tsp. fresh rosemary
1 tsp. fresh thyme
1 tbsp. fresh parsley chopped
1 tbsp. fresh basil, minced
10 olives, pitted and halved
Olive oil to taste

Salt and pepper to taste
Goat's yogurt (or any yogurt)
Fresh tomato wedges (optional)
Slices of bread (optional)
- Wash greens, spin dry and place in large salad bowl
- Add the rest of the ingredients, except yogurt.
- Toss with olive oil to taste
- Serve with a generous dollop of yogurt, and optional tomato wedges and bread slices on the side.

SIMPLE SALAD
½ head iceberg lettuce
½ head Romaine lettuce
3 tomatoes sliced in wedges
1 onion halved and sliced thin
Olive oil and vinegar, salt and pepper to taste
- Mix all ingredients together, tossing olive oil, vinegar, salt and pepper to coat evenly.
This simple salad compliments complex meals perfectly.

CHILLED GREEN BEAN SALAD
1 ½ lbs. fresh green beans just picked from the garden (if possible).

½ cup olive oil
½ cup chopped onions
1/3 cup vinegar
Salt and pepper to taste

- Split green beans lengthwise and then in half.
- Cook quickly in fast, salted boiling water until tender but not limp, about 1 or 2 minutes.
- Drain and spin dry.
- Toss beans in salad bowl with remaining ingredients.
- Chill and serve.
- Feta crumbled on top of this salad works well. So does the addition of olives.

Chapter Eight

VEGETABLES

From my great uncle's garden, you could pull together a feast in a matter of minutes – all fresh, all lively and colorful, all flavorful.

In a small, postage stamp size yard, he grew lemon, orange, fig and grapefruit trees. Climbing over the fence and arching over the walkway were his grapes, hanging lush and seductive under the hot sun. These would end up as a sweet red wine, without the additives found in commercial wines. Here, too, he grew peaches and pears, cabbages, tomatoes, all sorts of beans and lettuce. He augmented his nutrition, as all the Islanders do, with the wild greens that crowded his garden alongside his cultivated crops, and hedged in the parameters of his house. Peppers, eggplants, and corn completed the fare. There was just enough room for the walkway to his front door. No one really mows their lawn, here. If there is land that can be used to grow things – then things are grown. You cannot eat grass. Let the mountain goats forage on the hill tops where gardens are an impossibility – but the garden belongs to man. He basked in his largely domesticated vegetation and enjoyed a life of casual living, never straining much for his sustenance after the garden had been seeded. After all, the hot springs at Therma were not going to come to you. My grandmother, on the other hand, sought out challenges like a Navy Seal.

My grandmother often took me out to forage with her for that day's supper, because tomatoes and eggplant were, oh, so predictable. Whether in New York or in Ikaria, she insisted I be her shadow and catch the wild greens her eyes may have missed. She was like a Wall St. Banker who, not content with the mountain of gold bullions under his feet, felt the call of the wild to hunt down that one extra penny. You can't make a dollar out of 99 cents, after all.

In Ikaria I followed her agile steps up winding mountainous paths, plucking green gold from the earth. It was an all-day affair, because, of course, there was tea to be had with friends and family along the way.

My grandmother was a mountain goat. I, decades younger, struggled to keep pace with her. She exhilarated in the tops of peaks, and I heaved to prevent a stroke. I thought, if I died here, I would wish to be reincarnated as a slinky.

My grandmother taught me never to enter a friend's house empty-handed. You must always bring something with you to share or give outright as a gift. This is a funny little custom that my grandfather played with once. We were at the café and a cousin of his (they are mostly all cousins), offered him a book. My grandfather, knowing the custom of expressive generosity, even if it is not meant wholeheartedly, declined the kind offer, at which time the cousin offered the book more enthusiastically. It was obvious to me that the cousin did not want to part with the book, but encouraged by my grandfather's gentle rejection of the gift, found an opportunity to display his generosity all the more fervently to all who were watching. Again, my grandfather, knowing his cousin really wanted to keep the book, smiled and declined more forcefully, to do him a favor. Buoyed by my grandfather's further refusal, the cousin thrust the book into my grandfather's chest, adamantly declaring for all to hear that my grandfather really must have the book. It was his supreme pleasure to gift him the book. He insisted. My grandfather looked at me, winked, said, "Watch this," then looked his cousin, stretched out his hand and said, "OK" and took the book. The cousin was stunned that my grandfather would actually be brazen enough to accept the gift, and his pained expression now followed the book with longing.

"Well, if you didn't really want to give it to me, why did you insist on giving it to me? This is a very stupid tradition." The tradition of generous hospitality had morphed into a social statement, which looked very odd to the outsider.

And so, knowing people expect you to bring things to them when you see them, even while insisting that you should not have brought them anything and making a public display of trying to return your gift so that you are not put out – my grandmother wisely thought that no one would think of returning a gift gotten free from the earth. She had me pick chamomile, wild mint and lemon balm by the bucket full, and we stopped off at friend's house, herbs in hand, for tea.

This friend/cousin who grew up with my grandmother smiled widely at our arrival. The door to the house was open anyway, and she ushered us in the front door and out again through the back to sit under the grape arbor, heavy with ripening purple grapes that cast long shadows against the afternoon sun. We sat there while the tea boiled, and then, under the arbor, drank the tea flavored with local wild honey. The ever present sea in the distance shimmered with lights of diamonds under the sun, temporarily blinding me.

And then the gossip. While men talked politics and sports, women talked other women. I understand that this is a universal thing, but the poor women who were being gossiped about should have been present to defend themselves. And then it occurred to me that these same women who were providing noshing material against their will were, themselves, most liking noshing on other unsuspecting women. Eventually my Yiayia must have also felt how cruel this was, and so she changed the subject to flowers. Yes. Flowers. It was innocuous enough a subject matter. And then the real talk began. Because much as they are loathe to admit it, women don't really enjoy talking about other women. They enjoy talking about something that is closer to their hearts, something that brings them joy and fulfillment, something that makes them feel more human – indeed, more feminine. And so the roses were discussed, and the yellow roses brought out and cut and given to my grandmother as a token of friendship, and they exchanged cultivation secrets and recipes for making rose perfume and rose jam or rose glycol

This was their game and they were on top of it. They owned it. We drank chamomile / lemon balm tea and wild honey from precious china cups with floral paintings, and we felt like the elite. The tea, some of the best tea I have ever tasted, was a gift from the island, free and clear. It was a statement not of material wealth, but familial wealth, of the circle of love – of rightful inheritance. It was an example of God's provision. Who needed packaged teas when growing free was the best tea one could imagine? And suddenly, it felt great to be alive, to feel the life of growing things and our relationship to them, and our relationship to each other. At such moments, you could feel the earth's pulse, and it coincided with your own.

We were to meet again at church, at the celebration of life, a remembrance feast celebrated by the entire village forty days after the death of a loved one, in this case, someone's aged husband. They eat boiled wheat berries soaked in honey to illustrate anabiosis – the flight from death to life, rebirth, new beginnings, and all partake outside by the churchyard or cemetery, between the sun and the deep blue sea, and under the hand of the wind as it stirs to life the hair on heads as if to remind us that yes, the soul still lives and still takes flight; and we have never quite been entirely separated by the thin veil of mortality.

We went home for the customary afternoon siesta and, that evening, enjoyed a dinner of freshly picked figs, two boiled eggs, a cup of yogurt cheese, coffee and a cup of goat's milk into which my grandmother put a scant teaspoon of sugar to sustain us for the rest of the evening. We had dinner dates at various houses – not really by appointment but by mutual understanding that one of the days would bring us to the doorstep of our hosts.

One such meal was reminiscent of my father's cooking.

MOUSSAKA
2 eggplants
2 onions, chopped
1 cup water
½ cup tomato paste
2 tbsp. parsley
2 eggs, well beaten
½ cup grated cheese
½ cup olive oil
¼ lb butter

1 lb chopped meat, (optional). Can substitute 1 lb. farmer's cheese.

½ cup bread crumbs

salt and pepper to taste

- Brown meat, if using, with olive oil
- Add water, tomato paste, parsley, butter, salt and pepper and let simmer for one hour or until paste is thickened.
- Peel and cut eggplants lengthwise into ¼ inch strips.
- Sprinkle with flour and sauté in olive oil or butter till golden brown.
- Add onion mixture and 2 tbsp. of bread crumbs. Mix well
- Sprinkle with breadcrumbs on a buttered baking dish
- Place half of eggplant slices in dish and spread half of onion (meat or cheese) mixture on eggplant slices.
- Add remaining eggplant and onion (meat or cheese) mixture alternately.
- Pour beaten eggs on top and spread evenly.
- Sprinkle with grated cheese and bread crumb mixture and bake at 325 degrees for half an hour or until golden brown.

RICE WITH ALMONDS AND SQUASH FLOWERS

1/2 cup rice

1 cup washed squash flowers that have never been sprayed by anything but rain water, chopped or left intact for dramatic flair

½ cup slivered or sliced almonds.

1 ½ cup of water

½ tsp. sea salt.

2 tbsps. butter or

1 tbsp. olive oil

Salt and pepper to taste.

- Brown rice in olive oil or butter until golden brown
- Add water and simmer till tender
- Sauté squash flowers in olive oil or butter. Sprinkle lightly with salt and pepper to taste.
- Toast almonds on pan in oven, set at 350 degrees till golden brown.
- When rice is cooked, place in bowl and toss with flowers and almonds.
- Serve with salad, tomatoes, modest chunks of feta cheese and, of course, homemade red wine

BAKED VEGETABLES AS A MAIN DISH

1 lb. potatoes peeled.

1 lb okra

1 lb summer squash

¼ cup parsley

1 lb. tomatoes

1 lb. onions

1 cup olive oil

1 sprig dill

Salt and pepper to taste

- Slice potatoes, onions, squash and okra. Arrange vegetables on top layer. Sprinkle dill and parsley between layers, as well as salt and pepper and olive oil.
- Add a little water and bake at 350 degrees for about one hour or until potatoes are tender.
- Remove from heat and sprinkle with olive oil.

EGGPLANT AND TOMATO PILAF

2 eggplants

2 cups long grain rice (not from the American south or anywhere cotton had been planted first, as the arsenic levels are high in this regional rice)

2 tsps. Salt, plus salt to taste

4 cups boiling water

1 cup olive oil or as needed to taste
1 onion chopped
2 large tomatoes, chopped
½ tsp. ground cinnamon
½ tsp. ground allspice
1 tsp. freshly ground pepper
2 cups hot water or tomato juice
Chopped fresh mint

- Peel eggplants and cut into ½ inch cubes.
- Place the cubes in a colander, salt lightly and toss gently to mix
- Let stand for about 1 hour to drain off the bitter juices
- Meanwhile, in a bowl, combine the rice with the 2 tsps. Salt and pour into the boiling water. Stir well and let stand until the water is cold.
- Drain the rice and rinse well under cool running water.
- Drain again and let stand aside.
- Rinse eggplant cubes with cool water, drain well and pat dry with paper towels.
- In a large sauté pan, over medium heat, warm 3 tbsps of olive oil.
- Working in 3 batches and adding 3 tbsps olive oil with each batch.

- Add the eggplant cubes and sauté until golden brown on all sides, about 5 minutes.
- Using a slotted spoon, transfer the cubes to paper towels to drain set aside.
- In a saucepan over medium heat, warm the remaining 3 tbsps olive oil. Add the onion and sauté until tender, about 8 minutes.
- Add the rice and cook, stirring until opaque, about 3 minutes. Add the tomatoes and cook, stirring for 5 minutes longer.
- Add the sautéed eggplant, cinnamon, allspice. Salt and pepper to taste. Stir well.
- Pour in the hot water or tomato juice, cover and cook over low heat till liquid is absorbed.
- Sprinkle with mint and serve.

FRIED EGGPLANT (or Zucchini)

2 or more eggplants
- Cut in thick slices, without peeling,
- Sprinkle with salt and dip in flour
- Slow fry in olive oil until golden brown and crispy
- Use with garlic sauce

LIVING (and eating), DELIBERATELY

SPINACH WITH RICE

1 lb. spinach (or a combination of Vleeta and
tender dandelion leaves)
2 onions, chopped
1 tbsp. Chopped parsley
1 tbsp. Chopped dill
1 cup rice
1/4 cup olive oil
salt and pepper to taste

- Sauté onions in oil until golden brown.
- Wash and drain spinach and add to onions.
- Add a ½ cup of water to mix (or more, depending on preference) and bring to boil
- Add parsley, dill and rice
- Stir, season to taste and allow to simmer till cooked.

BEAN PLAKI

1 lb. white, kidney or bean of choice
1 cup olive oil
2 tbsp tomato sauce or 4 fresh, whole
tomatoes
3 onions, sliced
2 carrots, diced
½ cup minced parsley
2 stalks celery, chopped

salt and pepper to taste
- Soak beans overnight.
- Change water and boil.
- Add olive oil, tomato paste or fresh shopped tomatoes, onions, carrots, parsley and celery.
- Cook until tender.
- Season with salt and pepper to taste.

SOUFIKO

1 pepper, seeded and chopped (or more if desired)
1 tbsp fresh oregano, chopped, or 2 tsp. dried oregano
1 tbsp. fresh, aromatic basil, or 2 tsp. dried
2 onions, chopped
2 tsp sea salt or to taste
3 garlic cloves, chopped
3 zucchinis, chopped – keep the green skin on
3 potatoes, peeled and chopped
4 tomatoes, chopped, retaining the skins (they are full of antioxidants)
¾ cup olive oil
- In a large, heavy (cast iron is best) frying pan to which 2 tlbsp. olive oil have been poured, place all the ingredients, heaviest

- first, layering right up to the top, and finishing with half of the oregano and basil.
- Pour 1/2 cup olive oil over the top of this, cover and cook on a slow fire till tender, stirring occasionally to prevent sticking.
- Remove from heat and top off with remaining oregano, basil, and olive oil.
- Serve on a large plate with thin slices of bread and red wine.

KIDNEY BEAN DELIGHT

1lb kidney beans, soaked overnight and drained
1 large onion, chopped
3 cloves garlic, chopped
5 chopped tomatoes
3 stalks celery
3 cups Vleeta and / or tender dandelion leaves, chopped
2 tbsps. crushed Rosemary
Fresh parsley sprigs
Olive oil
Salt and pepper to taste
- In a large pot, cook beans with the rest of the ingredients.

- When beans are tender, salt and pepper to taste, then remove from pot, drain, but keep the broth for use in other recipes.
- Spoon onto a serving dish, garnish with parsley and drizzle generously with olive oil.
- May be served beautifully on a bed of rice and accompanied with fresh tomatoes or fish – or both.

Why more veggies than fish?

But why are the islanders more vegetarians than fish eaters? I have a theory and it references the history of the island.

Oral history tells us as much as books and, in Ikaria, was the prime method family history was handed down from one generation to the next. Some were funny, some thought-provoking. This is one of the thought-provoking stories my father would tell us time and again during suppers.

We had a great-grandfather x ?, who, in the 17th century, was a young father of a three-year-old daughter. He was on his fishing vessel with his first mate and they were hauling the catch for the day when a dreaded pirate ship overtook them. After beheading the first mate and baptizing the ship with his blood, the pirates sold my great-grandfather as a slave in Africa and there he suffered the physical and mental torment any slave would suffer under the hands of brutal slaveholders. When he was liberated by the French nine years later and returned back home to Perdiki, he arrived in the midst of a funeral. Thin as a rail, broken in health and aged beyond his years, no one recognized him as he asked some of the villagers who the funeral was for. They answered, "It's the widow Lefas's daughter. Her only child. She was just twelve-years-old."

When the funeral was over, my great-grandfather made his way to his old home and knocked at the door. My great-grandmother answered – grief had nearly taken her voice. He introduced himself as her husband, but she did not recognize, nor believe him.

"How could you be so cruel as to come to me today, of all days, and tell me this? Don't you know I have just buried my only child? My husband was lost at sea nine years ago."

Here is where food became the key that unlocked her door of denial. He reminded her of the wine they had made together just before he vanished. It was such good wine of uncommonly good quality, that they hid it in a special place in the cellar so they could keep it all to themselves and share only the lesser quality wine with guests. She looked at him and realized that no one could have known this but her husband – for even she had never mentioned it to anyone and had, indeed, not thought of it in years. She then opened her heart and home to him, they had more children, and I am here writing about it because she believed him. But he also never went to sea to fish again. Instead, oral history has it that he sustained himself and his family solely from their garden and orchard, and, I suspect, had a few goats or chickens in their barn as well.

SPRING BOUNTY

To make a simple dish of cooked Vleeta, Dandelion or Lamb's Quarters greens, or all three combined Mediterranean style, gather enough greens to fill a gallon pot (or more, depending on the number of people to be served).

- Remove the stems from the leaves and wash.
- Steam just until limp and tender.
- Sprinkle with olive oil, lemon juice, salt and pepper to taste.
- Dill, oregano and parsley enrich the already amazing flavors.

Goes very well with any seafood dish or stands triumphantly on its own.

Chapter Nine

SOUPS

LENTIL SOUP

1 lb. lentils
½ cup olive cup
1 cup chopped celery
1 cup chopped Vleeta or young dandelion
leaves, when in season
½ cup diced carrots
5 fresh tomatoes, diced. OR two cans diced
tomatoes.
2 cloves garlic
3 medium size potatoes (organic or home-
grown), peeled, diced.
1 tbsp each oregano, basil and parsley, if dry,
and as much as you can handle if fresh.
Dash of ginger
Dash of mustard, to taste
Salt, pepper to taste

- Wash and sort lentils (to remove any wayward stones), and add to cooking pot with all ingredients.
- Cover with about 2 quarts of water or until all vegetables are covered by at least 2 inches, or more, of water.
- When soup begins to boil, lower fire and let simmer until tender.
- Add salt and pepper to taste. Add ginger and mustard if desired (for an extra kick).

CHICK PEA SOUP (REVITHIA)

1 lb. chick peas
½ cup olive oil
2 large onions chopped
Salt and pepper to taste.

- Soak chick peas overnight
- When ready to cook Rinse well and rub peas between fingers to remove as many skins as possible.
- Rinse again and put to boil with water to cover.
- Simmer until almost tender, adding more hot water if necessary. Add chopped

- onions, oil and seasoning and cook until done.

HEARTY BEAN SOUP

1 pound of any dried beans of your choice – lentils, kidney, white navy, etc, or all varieties together
½ cup barley or rice
1 large onion, diced
2 cloves garlic, diced
6 fresh tomatoes (or one can diced tomatoes)
1 quart homemade tomato soup (or two cans processed tomato soup)
3 stalks celery, diced
3 carrots, diced
1 fistful fresh parsley, or 2 tbsp. dried parsley
5 leaves fresh basil – or to taste. Or 1 tbsp dried basil
2 fistfuls of fresh, young, tender dandelion leaves (or leafy vegetable of your choice), chopped
Salt and pepper to taste
Splash of olive oil

- Soak beans overnight. Drain. (Lentils need not be soaked overnight.)
- Place beans with vegetables and herbs in pot. Do not put salt in until after beans

- have cooked as putting salt in the beginning will toughen the beans and vastly prolong cooking time.
- Cook until beans are tender and broth is rich. Be careful not to scorch.
- Once beans are cooked, it is safe to add salt and pepper.
- Add water if desired to obtain soup consistency you wish
- Add olive oil for flavor

Serve on bed of pasta, or cooked barley or rice, or alone with a wedge of bread and a few slices of fresh tomatoes. And, as always, red wine tops off this hearty meal.

WHITE BEAN OR LIMA BEAN SOUP or VEGATBLE DISH WITH WILD SPRING GREENS

1 lb of white beans or lima beans

1 gallon dandelion, lamb's quarters and vleeta greens (chicory leaves also if they have been prepared by boiling them, rinse off the water and boiling again, to remove any bitter taste)

Green tops of young, wild scallions

2 tsps of either rosemary, basil or dill – or throw caution to the wind and put in all three.

Juice of one lemon (optional)

2 tblsp olive oil.

- Soak beans overnight and pour off water.
- Place beans, rosemary, basil and wild spring greens with scallion tops in pot to boil.
- Cook till tender.
- Salt and pepper to taste.
- If using as a soup, retain the water and pour in lemon juice (optional) and olive oil.
- If using as a vegetable dish, drain water (but keep for other recipes), and toss with lemon juice and olive oil.

SAVORY TOMATO SOUP

2 onions, chopped
2 cloves of garlic, minced
1 small cucumber, peeled, seeded and coarsely chopped
2 lbs ripe, fresh tomatoes cut in quarters.
2 small green bell peppers, seeded, chopped, (optional)
6 tbsps. olive oil (optional)
2 tbsps. dried or ¾ cup fresh, chopped parsley
2 tbsps. fresh Rosemary.
2 tbsps. fresh basil
Sugar, Salt and freshly ground pepper to taste

- In a large pot, cook all ingredients except parsley until done. Let cool.
- When cool, place soup in blender and blend until smooth.
- Pour soup back into pot via a sieve to eliminate the seeds.
- Place parsley into soup and cook until parsley is tender.
- Serve
- Garnish with fresh parsley.

May be served with Dolmades for a satisfying meal.

OKRA STEW

1 lb. okra
2 onions, chopped
1 cup stewed tomatoes
½ cup olive oil
½ cup water
juice of ½ lemon
2 tbsp chopped parsley
- sale and pepper to taste
- Wash and trim okra.
- Sprinkle with lemon juice and let stand 20 minutes
- Prepare sauce by frying chopped onions lightly in olive oil

- Add stewed tomatoes and water
- Add parsley and simmer a little longer
- Drain okra and place in casserole into which half the tomato sauce has been placed on the bottom
- Cover with the rest of the sauce.
- Season to taste.
- Cover and simmer gently or bake in moderate oven till okra is tender.

PAPA'S SIMPLE SPLIT PEA SOUP

1 lb. split peas
2 onions, chopped
salt and pepper to taste
Olive oil to taste

- Soak split peas overnight.
- Discard water and cook with onions till tender.
- When tender, add salt and pepper to taste
- Remove from heat and sprinkle with olive oil to taste.

GARLIC – FOR MEDICINAL PURPOSES

My father ate onions like they were apples. His eyes glistened. His countenance glowed. This, he exclaimed, was food fit for the gods.

Though he kept his onion preferences to himself, he made sure to share his belief in garlic as the cure-all with his progeny. Of course we now know that garlic has been shown to have anti-bacterial and anti-fungal properties, lowering blood pressure, cholesterol and the risk of infections, and acts as a blood thinning agent, combating stroke and heart disease. It also strengthens the immune system.

My father did not possess the results of clinical studies that illustrated these qualities, but he did have empirical evidence – his own life. And he, as any good father, was duty bound to pass on that advantage to us.

Whenever we, as children, were sick, my father would come into the room armed with a glass of water in one hand and a clove of garlic in the other. He would encourage – no, command us to eat the garlic. He was certain it would heal us. He was amazingly correct. As soon as we saw him coming with his arsenal, we immediately experienced miraculous healing. Undaunted by our instant recovery, he still insisted that we chew the clove thoroughly and swallow it, washing it down with the water. He did not leave our sides until we had ingested that pungent bulb. And, indeed, we were always better by morning. At least he spared us the straight-up olive oil.

BLACK EYE PEAS WITH OLIVE OIL AND GARLIC

1 lb. black eye peas
1 onion, diced
4 cloves garlic, diced
2 cups chicken broth, optional
4 ripe tomatoes, diced
2 stalks celery, diced
2 carrots, diced
2 sweet peppers, diced and seeded
2 tbsp. Basil
½ tsp fennel
½ tsp. cumin
1 cup Vleeta – Lamb's Quarters, if in season, chopped
1 cup young, tender dandelion leaves, if in season, chopped
2 – 4 tbsps. olive oil, as per personal preference
Salt, pepper to taste

- Soak black eye peas overnight
- Drain peas, add to large pot.
- Add the rest of the ingredients, sans salt and pepper

- Add enough water to cover vegetables – plus several inches.
- Boil at a steady boil until vegetables and peas are tender
- Add salt, pepper and olive oil

Can be served as a soup or cooked down and served as a vegetable medley.
Serve with a hearty bread, salad and wine.

My mother, like me, was more American than Ikarian. Yes, her parents came from the Ikarian village of Oxea and yes, she married my father from Perdiki, but her tastes were different, having been raised in Brooklyn and mingled, as she did, with the Jewish, Polish and Italian people that populated Pacific St. during that time. But one thing she made, true to her island roots, was Chicken Lemon Soup or Avgolemeno Soupa. It varied every time with the making, just as Yiayia's stories, but it was always delicate, always mouth-watering and it never failed.

Here is one version of her soup that my father was happy to take a backseat to.

MAMA'S AVGOLEMENO SOUPA
(Αυγολέμονο Egg and lemon soup with chicken)

This soup has a rich taste with just the right amount of tang; savory and satisfying on a cold winter evening.

1 Good whole chicken 2-3 pounds
Enough water to completely cover the chicken in a large (4 quarts or more) pot
3 stalks celery, diced
One or two large onions (depending on taste), diced
Two cloves of garlic, diced
3 carrots, diced
2 eggs
Juice of one lemon
1 tsp. Basil (preferably fresh), 3 tbsp of fresh
1 tbsp Parsley (preferably fresh)
½ tsp. Oregano (preferably fresh)
½ tsp sage
Salt and pepper to taste
1/2 cups cooked Rice (optional)
- Boil together all ingredients but rice until a good, hearty broth develops. Remove from heat. Remove chicken from pot. It

should be very tender and the meat should fall away from the bones readily.

- Place the meat back into the pot.
- (I let the soup cool enough so that the fat forms a layer on top. I skim off most of the fat, but leave some for flavor.)
- Take one cup of the broth and set aside.
- In another cup, whisk together the 2 eggs.
- Pour the eggs into the cup of broth, whisking while doing so. This keeps the cooked eggs from clumping into balls and strands.
- Pour egg mixture back into pot while whisking vigorously.
- Squeeze the juice from the 2 lemons and add to pot.
- Traditionally, soup is strained so that only the broth is left.
- Save the vegetables as a side dish, or, if desired, leave in soup for a hearty version of Chicken Lemon Soup.

Leftovers may be frozen until a later date. Lemon juice may have to be added when serving the leftovers to reconstitute the full flavor.

Chapter Ten

THE LESSONS

My mother percolated my father's coffee while pressing me into service to set the table for supper. My father's hands almost always smelled of chicken after work. It was a popular menu item, and he would laugh, drink slowly from his cup and wait for supper in a good-humored calm. Whatever was put on our kitchen table, it had to be accompanied with olives, onion, garlic and wine. I have seen my father in less refined moments, biting into a whole, raw onion as if it were an apple and swallow it down with a swig of olive oil followed by wine to cleanse his palate. The man never had a stroke.

The table had a smooth white and gray laminated top. On this were placed heavy duty restaurant dishes, courtesy of the surplus from my grandparents' restaurant. My father sat at the head of the table under the Roman numeral clock. We sat wherever we could get a seat. At six o'clock the lessons began. Supper, when my father was around, was incidental.

"Pericles," my father would begin the art of illumination, "was a brilliant general and leader, the most brilliant Greece ever knew." And with that segue, he began to pull together everyone's silverware, cups and dishes. I was about to put salt on my food when my father snatched the salt shaker out of my hand.

"And this," he declared as he held up the salt shaker like it was a prized lottery ticket, "is the ship in Piraeus, as is this," he snatched up the pepper shaker from my brother's hand.

We watched in silence as he arranged the shakers around the silverware he had lined up and had us relive the battle of Piraeus. The clever naval strategies of the ancients never ceased to amaze and amuse him and, in turn, us. He retold history with a liveliness that made television look dull and unintelligent. Forks and knives became fleets of ships, ketchup bottles on their sides became craggy ports, and if the table surface itself was not the ocean, then it represented the places where the people whose livelihoods and histories were shaped by the ocean, and whose blood was ever connected to the sea, lived, and etched their own stories into the eternal web of human history.

There is something about urban legends, folk lore and stories that the islanders love, in fact, judging from my father, even thrive on. My father was a great story teller. He had stories of fairies and pirates and angels. He had stories of his father's and his own early days as immigrants to this new world, of the patience and eternal kindness of his mother, of human mischief and crafty animals. Supper time was not a time to eat so much as it was a time to hear a story told by the master himself.

"Dionysus," he was fond of saying, "walked all over Greece with a lantern held high, looking for an honest man."

"Did he really?" I would ask, for it seemed silly to me that a man would need a lantern in the daylight as well as the night.

My father would only laugh and say, "And he still hasn't found him. And Socrates, who never wrote a book, was the greatest philosopher of all time because he did not tell you what to think; he asked questions and let your own answers be your guide to understanding."

I thought this a novel approach to teaching, and wished the pastor or my teacher would adopt it. And when my mother was angry at something we had done, it would have been infinitely better had she questioned us into illumination rather than the usual alternative.

While the food got cold and my father tutored us in philosophy and Archimedes, the world outside dissolved, muted out, and all I could see were the temples and gymnasiums, and St. Paul preaching on Mars Hill on the rock in the market place by the Parthenon, for my father loved to bring St. Paul into all the treasures of Greece.

My father's name was Philipos, and his accent was so thick, none of my friends could understand him when he spoke English. Tall and lean like his fellow islanders, he came to this country with the knowledge of how to make soap, cheese and wine. A naive farm boy of twenty-one with close-cropped hair and a defiant expression, his dark, intense eyes blaze out from his passport photo. Those eyes took on a soft glow by the time I was old enough to recognize my Papa.. He treated his children with dignity and respect, and that alone taught us more than all his words. We were sad whenever we upset him, but we were never afraid.

My father came to this country in the middle of the Great Depression. There he reunited with a father he had seen but once since he was born, a father who walked right past him at Ellis Island because he did not recognize him. From there my father landed his first job shining shoes in Grand Central station for a dime. Every time I walk past the big clock in the center of the station, I think of my father glancing up at it to check what time he had to get back to his father's apartment in Brooklyn. From there he worked at the old Horn and Hardart automats and then, learned how to cook. Why not? He was Greek. He later cooked for the Army, and when he was discharged, he cooked for restaurants, becoming head chef at some of Manhattan's finest. In time, the aroma of his culinary masterpieces would flatten the stank and smog curling up from the tenements and make friends out of unlikely passers-by. His leg of lamb, soaked in wine and drenched in garlic and herbs, was so powerful and enticing a bouquet, it often neutralized warring factions and paralyzed enemies and friends alike with sudden and irreversible salivation. Anything he cooked released a potent aromatic, gastronomic tour de force throughout the entire apartment complex we lived in as if begging all to stop in their tracks, whether for good or evil, and imagine what the world would be like if all God's people could sit around a table offering whatever it was my father was cooking. It drew people to our door in droves. The mailman had no extra mail for us but, hey, what was that wonderful smell? Friends dropped by, just to 'touch base.'

The most grateful man to come to our door lived on the third floor. His name was Andy. He was the building's drunk, but he was the most obliging, kindly, thoughtful drunk I had ever met. He loved my father and he loved my father's cooking. By the time I first met him, he was already a broken man, but I did not know it then. He suffered what too many people suffer; a very low self-esteem and the inability to understand how to support his family. His wife was a proud and highly intelligent woman and it was she who worked to make certain their two boys had everything they needed to get ahead. She didn't pull any punches, and she made no excuses for herself. She was not adverse to hard labor and she loved children to excess. She loved them with a devotion that was iron-clad and guaranteed. And nothing, not even a drunk husband, was going to usurp that love. Andy's wife loved her husband, too, but his drinking continuously made her embarrassed, then sad, and then angry and finally, indifferent.

Andy had his shortcomings, and he knew it. But he was, by nature, a kindly sort with that one glaring weakness, and whenever he smelled my father's cooking, he became the most affable soul you could ever meet. That is the way I remember him most; warm, sincere, affable, and saturated with drink. And this is how he appeared when he would knock on our door after having been led by his nose.

My father genuinely liked the old man. We could smell his liquor as unmistakably as he could smell our kitchen, but my father, still under the influence of his island upbringing, put hospitality above all else. He also understood something of the pride of men and the broken spirit of Andy, and he would graciously meet him at the door and let him in for a bite to eat. The conversation of the two of them, a drunk and a Greek who was still not comfortable with the English language, became commonplace.

"Mizzter Phil, 'cha doin'?"

"Achoo, Andy, chew down?"

"No chew down, 'cha doin' Whaz 'achoo'?"

"Who chews? Ah! Chews! You wants chews some food?"

"No Mizzter Phil, how cha' doin'?"

"Oh, how cha – oh yes, and how you?"

"You sure iz nize, Mizzter Phil. Nize man. Yessiree."

"Stank you, Andy. You good man, too. You come in forrr to eat? Yes?"

"Naw, I couldn', but, hey, no I couldn'."

"Come. You like. Is nice leg of lamb."

"You too nize, Mizzter Phil."

"Is good for you. You sit here. Troy! Eat!"

"Well, thaz so nize, Mizzter Phil. You sure iz nize."

And Andy would sit down and we would all gather round and watch him eat. He would eat with complete gratitude, take a bite, smile at my father, take another bite, smile back, affirm my father's good standing, and polish off everything on his plate. It is not that his wife did not cook for him. She cooked until her kids were plump and she was proud. It is just that Andy needed a man who understood him, at least a man who did not condemn him or judge him. I think he came not so much for the food as for the acceptance. He did not need to be reminded of how the drink forced him to abdicate his paternal role. In my father's company, he found sanctuary.

My father could turn a roast leg of lamb into a spiritual epiphany. The aroma of that roast alone could sedate you into next week. It was seductive, delectable, tantalizing and the golden scepter of familiar gatherings. It was reserved for special Sundays – and always Easter Sunday, or Paska. It was marinated in homemade wine from the night before where my father lovingly bathed it and encouraged it with minced garlic and salt. That was all that he needed. By the time it came out of the oven after church on Sunday, it was a fragrant homage to the old country, to family love and to the peace and joy that being together meant. It was my favorite meal of all time.

When I lived in Greece with my uncle and cousins and saw the Paska lamb whom I had befriended on the roasting spit slowly turning over an open flame in the front yard, I vowed never to eat lamb again. Yet that cannot divest from me the memory of my father's cooking, for it was not an act of eating then, but an act of love that gathered us all around the table for conversation, togetherness and his incomparable cuisine.

He didn't cook with exact measurements – only intuition. Here, as close as I can get to the measurements he used, is his recipe for Leg of Lamb – Paska style.

PAPA'S LEG OF LAMB
A leg of lamb, fresh if possible.
A bottle of good red wine
One bulb of garlic
One onion

Sea salt

- Wash the leg of lamb.
- Cut slits into the leg and insert a clove of garlic in each slit
- Rub gently with sea salt to taste.
- Place leg of lamb in roasting pan and pour wine over it. Turn it every two hours then cover and let it soak in the wine overnight.
- Remove covering.
- Garnish leg and pan with sliced onions and basil leaves, fresh if possible.
- Place in moderate oven.
- Cook until tender and done.
- Savor.

Good accompaniments:

A humble salad with greens, tomatoes, onions, and tossed with vinegar and olive oil.

Braised Green Beans in butter and minced onion.

Plain rice, brown or white, tossed with parsley and basil.

Sides: Sliced tomatoes

Slices of feta cheese.

If necessary, sliced bread, though bread is usually not eaten with the meal.

A good red wine, sweet or dry but preferably homemade.

Chapter Eleven

BREADS

Bread is not a staple at every meal in Ikaria as it is elsewhere. Rather, it is an occasional accompaniment. And while there are plenty of plain bread recipes to be had from mainland Greece, I thought I would share the more fancy ones here since bread is an infrequent guest at Ikarian meals; and if you are going to be an infrequent guest, you might as well be stunning during those rare times you do show up.

ORANGE SWEET BREAD
1 cup milk
½ cup orange juice

2 tsp cinnamon
½ cup water
1 tsp. orange rind
2 pkgs. Yeast
1 tbsp. baking powder
2 cups sugar
1 cup butter, melted (or oil)
4 eggs
1 tbsp. salt
5-7 cups of flour – at least enough to make a soft dough

- Heat milk, orange juice and cinnamon together and cool to lukewarm
- Mix yeast into liquid mix and stir – then set aside.
- In a large mixer bowl (preferably one with a kneading hook) place butter and sugar and cream together.
- Add eggs and continue to cream
- Add the yeast mixture and orange rind and mix well.
- Mix in remaining ingredients – all but the flour.
- Using a dough hook, slowly pour the flour into the liquid mix in the bowl and stir well, one cup at a time, until an elastic dough is formed.

- Knead by machine (or by hand if no machine is available) until soft, elastic and pliable.
- Cover and let rise in a warm place.
- Knead again, then shape into desired shapes of circles, braids, or place in loaf pans.
- Brush top with beaten egg for a nice glossy finish
- Bake at 325 degrees till golden and bottom sounds hollow when tapped.

PASKA, OR EASTER BREAD

2 cups warm milk
2 pkg. yeast
1 tsp salt
8 eggs, beaten
½ cup melted butter or cooking oil
¼ cup sugar
6-7 cups sifted flour

- Pour yeast, sugar and warm milk into large mixing bowl and mix, then let stand.
- Beat eggs and pour into mixture.
- Add salt.
- Slowly add flour until the dough is thick.
- Knead with dough hook (or by hand) until elastic.

- Lay dough on table and roll into one long rope.
- Cut into three equal pieces
- Beginning at one end, braid the three pieces then join the end to the beginning, making a round wreath.
- My family adds three red dyed eggs into the completed bread before it has risen.
- Allow to rise to nearly double in size.
- Brush top with beaten egg for glaze.
- Bake at 325 degrees till done, about half an hour to 45 minutes.

SWEET BREAD

2 cups milk, heated
½ lb. butter, melted, cooled
1 tbsp salt
2 tsp. vanilla
1 ½ tsp anise extract - optional (could also use orange or almond)
6 eggs, beaten
1 ½ cups sugar
1 pkg. yeast
5-7 cups flour

- Dissolve yeast and sugar in the two cups warm milk in large mixing bowl

- Add beaten eggs, butter, salt and anise extract, if using.
- Add flour slowly, one cup at a time, until a stiff dough is formed.
- Knead by hand or with dough hook until soft and elastic.
- Form into desired shape (disks, loaves or braids) and allow to rise in a warm, undisturbed place.
- Brush with beat egg for glaze
- Bake at 325-350 degrees until golden. Do not over bake.

ORANGE BREAD WITHOUT YEAST

2 ½ lbs. flour
10 eggs, separated
1 ½ cups sugar
½ lb butter, melted
1 tsp. baking soda
1 tsp. baking powder
Juice of 10 oranges
Grated rind of one orange

- Beat egg yolks
- Add sugar, a little at a time until dissolved.
- Melt butter, add to mixture and beat until smooth.

- In a separate bowl, mix orange juice with baking soda and baking powder.
- In another bowl, beat egg whites till stiff, but not dry.
- Add flour into the egg yolk mixture, a little at a time, alternating with the orange juice mixture until complete.
- Fold in the stiffly beaten egg whites.
- Pour batter in greased baking pan of desired shape.
- Bake at 325-350 degrees for 30 – 35 minutes or till cake pulls away from sides of pan.

ORANGE NUT BREAD

1 medium sized orange, juiced, retaining rind.
Boiling water (enough to make one cup when added to orange juice)
1 cup pitted dates
2 tbsp. melted butter
1 tsp. vanilla
1 egg, beaten
2 cups flour
¼ tsp. salt
1 tsp. baking powder
½ tsp baking soda
¾ cup sugar

½ cup chopped nuts
- Place juice and pulp from orange in measuring cup and fill with boiling water to make one cup.
- Pour into mixing bowl
- Cutting out the white sheath of the skin, place orange rind and dates through a food processor. These, together, should measure one cup.
- Add orange and date mixture to liquid in mixing bowl.
- Blend in melted butter, vanilla and beaten egg and beat till incorporated.
- Sift flour, salt, baking powder, soda and sugar together, and blend into fruit mixture.
- Add nuts.
- Pour into well-greased and floured loaf pan.
- Bake at 350 degrees for about an hour and a half or till toothpick comes out clean.

Paxamathia

Paxamathia – or dried bread – was a staple at my grandparents' home both in New York and Ikaria.

In the old days before refrigeration, leftover bread was allowed to dry, just like biscotti, and then secured and stored for casual eating later. It used to be made of just plain bread, but as wars ceased and times became more prosperous, Paxamathia evolved much as biscotti did, and special breads are now made with anise, cinnamon or grated lemon rinds to add flavor to a staple that always promises some type of food supply and refreshments for guests in the pantry, no matter the season.

My grandparents, however, made their Paxamathia the old way – out of unused day-old breads. My grandmother would slice the breads in pieces, allow them to dry overnight in a very low oven, then pack them into tins. When company came, out came the tins and the Greek Coffee and the gossip and the politics and the stories and the laughter. These plain old pieces of dry bread, dunked in coffee, seemed anything but plain old pieces of dry bread. They seemed like a delicious rare treat that could only be enjoyed when company came, and the way the company dug in, these dry pieces of bread looked downright delicious.

Some of the sweet breads mentioned in this section could be delicious as Paxamathia, used in the same way as biscotti.

Chapter Twelve

DESSERTS

"And we heard knocking at the door for the third time," Yiayia explained carefully over a dense cup of Greek coffee.

We all leaned in closer, ignoring the sticky layers of baklava and halvah piled high in the center of the table in honor of my grandmother's visit, She had just returned from Ikaria.

Yiayia's sharp, sky-blue eyes looked at my parents and brothers, in turn, as we strained to hear every dramatic word sharply accentuated with an accent as pronounced as feta cheese.

Yiayia leveled her gaze on us; solemn, knowing, nodding her head somberly with the wisdom of her years, and held her peace. Us children dared not breathe. We caught our breath and did not let a wisp escape until Yiayia saw fit to relieve us with illumination. It was agony. My father, dark as she was fair, with the same finely chiseled nose as my grandmother, though they were only in-laws to each other, leaned even closer, the upper half of his body now hovering over the table, his shirt dangerously close to the lemon honey syrup that coated the baklava. He, like his countrymen, possessed a passion for the vibrant, oral folklore tradition of the island, a tradition that did not let practicality, or science, deprive them of a good story. His impatience got the best of him.

"And, Mama, tell us. You heard a knock for the third time," he burst.

"And then," my grandmother laid down her cup on the saucer with a sharp release, and looked at us with a keen, swift, incisive glance, carving out our incredulity like a lancet, "the knocking continued, but we were having such a loud time at your cousin Thanasie's house and barely heard the knocking. It was persistent, like the moo of a cow just before milking. You Papa, he said, 'Answer the door, Thanasie! See who it is."

I could hear myself sweat.

"So, Thanasie, he opened the door. And there stood his neighbor Elias.

"'Come in, Elias, and have refreshments with us,' Thanasie said, " Yia-Yia continued. "But Elias did not move. So Thanasie demanded all the harder, 'I said, come in!' But Elias just stood there. Finally Elias spoke. 'Will you please go to my house and bury my body.' And that was all he said before he turned away and walked back to his house. We were all perplexed by Elias's strange behavior. So we decided to follow him, but he had already gone inside. And so we knocked. But the door was locked and he did not answer. When the men broke down the door, sure enough, there was Elias. He had been dead already for - three - days," She concluded, as if she really needed the dramatic pauses to impress us with the impact of the story.

The sighs and groans that flashed around the table sounded like a small earthquake.

"Do you really think it's true?" I asked my father when we were alone in the kitchen. As a chef, the cooking duties fell on him and supper was due soon.

My father looked far away, as if trying to put himself in his old home town that he had not see for thirty years.

"Yes, yes," he said slowly. "I believe it is."

Folklore or oral history is best said in the accompaniment of coffee and dessert. It's just the way it is. It goes hand in hand.

In order to enhance your own story telling, here are a few tried and true recipes to accompany your tall tales.

BAKLAVA
Syrup
1 ¼ cup sugar
1 ¼ cup water
2 tsps. lemon juice
2 tsps. Cinnamon
¼ cup honey

FILLING
1 ¼ lbs. (20 oz.) walnuts, pistachios or pecans
½ cup sugar
1 tsp. cinnamon
1 lb. sweet butter
1 lb. phyllo

- Prepare syrup by boiling the sugar, water, cinnamon, and lemon juice for 10 minutes. Add honey. Strain and set aside.
- Combine walnuts, sugar and cinnamon in a bowl.
- Melt butter in small pan. Butter a 10" x 14" baking pan. Place one phyllo sheet at a time, brushing with melted butter after every sheet. After third sheet, sprinkle

walnut filling and continue alternating with phyllo and filling until you have used the phyllo, ending with 5 or 6 sheets of phyllo for the top layer. Brush top generously with butter. Score in diamond shaped pieces.

- Bake at 359 degrees for 45 to 60 minutes or until golden brown. Pour cooled syrup over pan of baklava. Allow to cool and cut pieces diagonally through to serve.

ANCIENT GREEK CANDY (SOUTZOUKI)

2 pounds walnuts, shelled
8 pounds grapes.

- Thread a large, clean needle, with a double strand of sturdy thread about 16 inches long.
- String together the nut meats, like a popcorn and cranberry garland, making sure the nut meats are pushed closely together
- Wash and stem grapes.
- Put them through a food processor or, as in days of yore, press them through a colander which has been placed over a large pot to catch the juice, using the back

of a large wooden spoon to push them through.

- Boil the grape juice gently (there should be about a gallon) until it is reduced to about one pint.
- Suspend the string of nutmeats over the pot.
- Using a ladle or large spoon, pour the thickened juice down over the string of nutmeats. As soon as the grape juice hardens, repeat the process, coating all sides of the nutmeats.
- One pint of thickened grape juice is usually sufficient for two strings of walnut meats.
- Suspend coated walnut meats over the pot until the thickened grape juice has set. When sufficiently dry and set, the strings may then be cut in short 2 or 3 inch lengths, wrapped in wax paper and stored in an airtight container

CHEESE HONEY PIE

2 lbs. cottage cheese
1 cup honey
½ cup sugar
1 tsp. cinnamon
8 eggs

PASTRY

½ cup butter

1 ½ cups flour

1 tsp. salt

- Mix cottage cheese with sugar until fine in texture.
- Add honey and mix well
- Add eggs, one at a time and beat after each addition.
- Beat in cinnamon.
- For pastry, cut butter, flour and salt in bowl. Handle gently till all is incorporated and smooth, but do not overdo
- Line bottom of pan with pastry
- Pour cheese mixture on top and bake at 325 degrees for 30 minutes.
- Cool and sprinkle with sugar and cinnamon.
- Cut in diamond pieces.

ALMOND CAKE

12 eggs, separated

1 lb almonds, ground

2 cups sugar

1 tsp. baking powder

Grated rind of three lemons

Juice of ½ lemon

1 tsp. almond extract (optional)
- Beat egg yolks till fluffy.
- Carefully add sugar and cream well
- Add ground almonds, baking powder, lemon rind and almond extract
- Add lemon juice and mix.
- Beat egg whites till softly stiff
- Fold whites into egg yolk mixture until blended.
- Pour into greased baking pan and bake at 250 degrees for 45 minutes or until a toothpick inserted in middle comes out clean.
- Remove from over and allow to stand till semi cool
- Cut into squares or diamonds and pour syrup (recipe follows) over top of cut cake

SYRUP
2 cups sugar
1 cup water
Juice of 1/2 lemon
- Boil sugar and water together until syrup thickens – about 10 minutes.
- Remove from heat and pour in lemon juice.
- Return to heat for an additional five minutes or until syrup is the consistency of maple syrup.

Even though these goodies make tantalizing after dinner desserts – the best dessert I have ever eaten was a sweet watermelon just picked from the garden when the natural sugar content was very high. I would pass up cakes and baklava any day for a bite of the juicy, fresh watermelon, a perfect accompaniment to a hot day.

Chapter Thirteen

EASTER or "PASKA"

Most of Greek food circulates around holidays and Easter, or in Greek, Paska, is the highest and holiest holiday in Greece. It easily ellipses Christmas. It is entirely unlike American Greek Easters. Even here in this country, I can go to church on Saturday, hear the church bells ring at midnight, and go home to soup and sleep. But in Greece it is a mass social event. There, no man is an island. Fireworks begin to explode. Everyone spills outside the church with lit candles and, at the stroke of midnight, when the bells begin to peel riotously all across the land, everyone, friend and stranger, will greet you with a jubilant kiss and exclaim, "Christos Anesti!" "Christ is risen!"

The celebration is just beginning. All the next day is feasting, dancing, drinking and more dancing.

My grandmother came on Easter Sunday, not with chocolate Easter bunnies, but a basket full of Greek Easter cookies. It has been a staple in my home ever since. Add to the Easter eggs, dyed red to symbolize the blood of Christ and traditionally colored on Holy Thursday. The custom is for each person to grab hold of the egg on Easter, then crack the ends together with another person. Whosever egg remains uncrushed will . . . . I actually have no idea. I could never get a good answer from either of my parents.

GREEK EASTER COOKIES (KOULOURAKIA) version 1

1/2 lb. (2 sticks) unsalted butter
1 cup sugar
2 tbsp. baking powder
1 tsp. baking soda
4 oz. orange juice
1/2 tsp. vanilla extract
3 eggs
5 1/2 - 6 cups all-purpose flour
1 egg, beaten with a splash of vanilla extract
Sesame seeds

Red egg (optional)

- In the bowl, beat butter till soft. Add the sugar and continue to beat until light and fluffy.
- Add orange juice and vanilla extract. Add eggs one by one and mix until combined.
- Add baking powder and baking soda and continue to mix.
- Add flour carefully, one cup at a time.
- At the fifth cup of flour, proceed with caution. Test the dough. It should be elastic, but not sticky when rolling in your hands. If the dough is sticky, you can add more flour but know that you can also merely coat your hands with flour and roll it into shape then. You may also place it, covered, in the refrigerator for a few minutes to cool and make it easier to work with.
- Shape into little ropes around 6 inches long, and ½ inch in diameter.
- Fold each rope in half and twist ends around each other.
- Other shapes are braids or pinwheel shapes. My grandmother was fond of merely twisting the folded pieces together

- Brush with beaten egg for a nice golden finish.
- Sprinkle with sesame seeds (opt)
- Bake in a preheated oven at 350 degrees until golden brown (about 20 minutes).

KOULOURAKIA version 2

1 cup butter
2 cups sugar
7 large eggs, beaten
½ cup milk
5 Tbsp. baking powder
1 tsp. salt
1 tbsp. vanilla extract
9 1/2 cups flour
1 or 2 cups sesame seed (optional)

- Cream butter, add sugar and cream again.
- Add eggs and continue mixing
- Sift together dry ingredients and add carefully to mix, alternately with milk and flavoring.
- Knead till all ingredients are well incorporated
- Shape as ropes, loops with ends crossed over each other, or any shape desired.
- Carefully place each cookie on greased baking sheet.

- Brush with beaten egg for glaze
- Sprinkle sesame seed on top of each cookie, if desire.
- Bake at 350 till golden – about 15 – 20 minutes

SOFT KOULOURAKIA

12 egg yolks
1 cup orange juice
2 cups sugar
1 lb. butter (softened)
1 tsp. baking soda
5 tsp. baking powder
Vanilla, anise, orange, whatever taste sensation you desire
2 ½ lbs cake flour

- Beat butter till light and fluffy.
- In separate bowl, cream together egg yolks and sugar.
- Fold egg yolk and sugar mixture into creamed butter
- Add orange juice to egg / sugar / butter mixture and cream.
- Add flavoring.
- Add baking powder and baking soda to flour and pour into egg / sugar / butter mixture, one cup at a time, until the dough

is pliable and not sticky but easily shaped into desired shapes.

- Bake at 350 degrees till golden brown.
- While still warm, brush tops in a little water and roll in sugar and cinnamon, or sesame seeds.

KOURABIEDES (similar to Russian Tea Cakes)

1 cup butter
1/3 cup sugar
1 egg (or 2 egg yolks)
1 tsp. vanilla
2 cups flour
1 tsp. baking powder
1 tsp. cloves OR whole cloves
Confectioners sugar

- Mix together ingredients. Shape into small balls slightly larger than a walnut
- Bake at 350 degree until firm.
- If using whole cloves, omit the ground cloves and stick one clove in the middle of each cookie
- Roll in confectioner's sugar when cool.
- Cover and store in cool, dry place.

This cookie recipe could be easily altered by substituting almond extract and almond slivers for cloves and ground cloves. Lemon or orange could also be used. Actually, the variation on this theme is only limited to the imagination.

ORANGE DOUGHNUT BALLS (LOUKOUMADES)

2 tbsp. butter or shortening
¾ cup sugar
4 egg yolks ½ tsp. vanilla
1 tbsp grated orange rind
1 cup milk
4 tsp baking powder
1 ½ tsp. salt
3 cups flour

- Cream butter / shortening and sugar till fluffy
- Add egg yolks, vanilla and orange rind to mixture and continue to mix.
- Slowly pour in milk, baking powder and salt until well incorporated
- Add flour, one cup at a time.
- Beat until smooth.
- Drop batter by teaspoonful into deep, hot oil.
- Fry until golden brown.

- Drain on power towels and sprinkle with honey and cinnamon.
- Makes about 5 dozen

Chapter Fourteen

CHEESE

My father used to be in charge of the family goats and, while his father was in America making money to send back home, the duty of butchering them fell on him. He would slice the goat meat in slabs, wash the slabs, gather sea salt that had settled in rock crevasses by the sea and rub the salt into each piece of meat, then place the meat on the rock roof of the house to dehydrate under the obliging sun. When fully dehydrated, his mother would store the meat in wooden barrels to be hydrated as needed. This was before electricity, and refrigeration, came to the island in the 1960's. This is what helped keep the family from starvation during the world wars when, my father assured me, times were exceedingly lean. The family ate from their garden, their orchard of lemon and orange trees, their vineyard, their chickens, goats and on occasion, fish. Self-sufficiency was ingrained in my father like a tattoo.

Goats, however, as self-sufficient as the people who inhabit the island, are primarily prized for their milk and cheese that is made from their milk, more so than their meat.

SIMPLE GOAT CHEESE MADE WITH LEMON

1 quart goat's milk (NOT ultra-pasteurized)

1/3 cup fresh lemon juice (to curdle milk. This is in place of rennet. Vegetable rennet could also be used, and many prefer the firm result of this instead)

Salt (and herbs of your choice) to taste

- Use a stainless steel pot.
- Thermometer
- Wooden spoon or stainless-steel spoon to stir
- Cheesecloth
- Strainer

- Dowel or wood or stainless-steel spoon with a long handle (for propping the draining cheese)
- In a stainless steel pot, heat the milk slowly on the stove until it reaches 180 - 185 degrees. Remove from heat.
- Stir in lemon juice and allow milk sit for 10 minutes. You should see it begin to curdle, not unlike the way milk looks when you put vinegar in it to produce a buttermilk alternative.
- Pour milk mixture into a cheesecloth lined colander or strainer. Some people use sterile old pillow cases for this. Line a colander with two layers of cheese cloth.
- Pick up the edges of the cheese cloth, and tie the ends together – or use rubber bands to close. Make sure a bowl is beneath the colander, as you will want to catch the run-off, or whey, which can then be used in cooking later on.
- Hang the cheesecloth ball over the pot by using a wooden dowel, or long handled spoon, to thread through the rubber band top bundle.
- Brace the dowel over the edges of the pot where the cheese will drain. Let stand overnight.

- Scrape cheesecloth clean of cheese and place in glass bowl. Stir in salt and, if ambitious, herbs such as fennel, or minced lemon balm, or any other adventurous herb.
- Place cheese into a small bowl to shape it and squeeze gently, ridding it of more whey. Pat into a log shape, wrap in an airtight container and store in refrigerator.

FRESH YOGURT CHEESE

1 quart goat's milk (or whole cow's milk)
¼ cup yogurt, as starter, at room temperature

- Heat milk to just before a simmer – careful not to overheat.
- Mix yogurt in ½ cup of warm milk. Pour into jar or covered bowl. Wrap bowl or jar in a towel and let set undisturbed in a warm place for 12 hours or more. (A gas oven with a constant pilot is good for this)
- Place cheese in a large strainer or cheese cloth and drain.
- Add 1 tsp of salt or more to taste
- Store in glass jar in refrigerator. Great in tossed salads, omelets or as a spread.
- This cheese can be dressed with dill, rosemary, thyme or any herbs to infuse

- flavor. Lemon balm goes well and very refreshingly with this.

Chapter Fifteen

Interesting Side Notes That Have Nothing To Do With Food.

Because of the constant threat of pirates, venturing out to fish was very much like taking your life into your own hands and tempting the fates. Piracy was so prevalent and the inhabitants of Ikaria so wary of being prey, that they forbade dogs on the island for centuries, least the barking give the inhabitants away. Further, they had created a network of tunnels to augment the advantage they had in natural caves that crisscrossed the island, so that if a pirate landed in Agios Kirykos, the inhabitants could, via caves or tunnels under their homes, escape to Nas or Armenistis undetected. And safe. The topography of the island made staying alive under such relentless pirate sieges a possibility. You could walk across what seems like a level piece of land and suddenly smack your nose into a building that you had not seen from a mere twenty feet away. The mountaintop, visible as the island of Ikaria, is rich in unsuspecting dips and turns and houses were built deep in these crevasses so that no light from the homes could be seen from the sea, thus alerting pirates to the inhabitants' presence. A great-grandfather had, in the year 1800, built a church, St. George, in one such unexpected dip, and though standing in front of the church, you would not even notice that you were indeed hidden by the protective arms of the rocky terrain. I was walking with my grandfather along what I thought were merely rocks when this little church suddenly loomed in front of me out of nowhere. I was startled and my grandfather laughed. "Smart guy, your Papou, eh?"

But it gets even more interesting.

One of the most intriguing stories my father told concerned a group of villagers so isolated on the island that though most of the modern inhabitants have heard of them, many have never seen them. Reportedly, these isolated people still speak in Homeric Greek and still live in the ways of ancient Greece with tunics, speech and music. Recently I asked an elderly woman from Ikaria if this bit of folk lore were true – were there people who live on the island so remote from civilization that they have retained their ancient Greek ways? Yes, she affirmed. Those people, preserved as it were in time, do indeed still live in the ancient Greek tradition, isolated from the modern world and allowed to remain unmolested due to the craggy topography of the mountainous terrain they call home. She had, herself, searched them out in the midst of the pine forest and found one woman lifting water from a well – much as they would have 3,000 years ago. Even though the dialect the Ikarians speak retains a significant amount of classical Greek flavor because of their own isolation from the influx of civilization experienced by those on the mainland, my friend said she spoke with the woman briefly, and though comfortable with a number of classical terminologies, had a hard time understanding the woman at the well because of the staunchly Homeric word usage. The older Greeks were expected to learn Homeric Greek in school, which no doubt helped this elderly friend of mine converse, however haltingly, with this tunic-clad woman. They exchanged words briefly, each able to grasp the other's verbal intent, before parting ways. My father told me that during the Nazi occupation of the island during the war, a soldier, or scientist – here the account is fuzzy – discovered these unique people during his exploration of the island. But the Ikarian people, out of respect, have left these anachronistic peoples as they wish to be left – in peace.

PAPOU and the Meaning of Life

My grandfather had adjusted so well to American life that he became punctual for everything. I always suspected this was to exact revenge on someone for something someone never did because they couldn't respect a clock. Whatever it was that drove him to this oddity of exacting punctuality, this meticulous dedication to appointment keeping, is the stuff of modern mythology. The fact remains that he pursued it with an almost pathological passion (or so his fellow Ikarians would have us believe). In fact, he exceeded his punctuality – he usually liked to arrive earlier than the appointment. So early, he preferred to speed to get there. He once passed a red light in unleashed urgency and my father, who sat in white knuckled terror beside him yelled, "Papa, you passed a red light!"

My grandfather yelled back, "Well, what did you want me to do? Take it with me?"

My father, who used to smoke at the time, said he swallowed his cigarette whole.

A postman, evangelical by nature, used to stop by the restaurant and preach to my grandfather about his soul and eternal salvation. My grandfather would caramelize his onions, cook his menu orders, and listen with a slight smile on his face, but not say a word.

One day the post man asked, "So, Louie, what do you think about the hereafter?"

My grandfather thought for a brief moment, then said while keeping his eye on the stove, "It must be pretty good – I've never heard of anybody coming back and complaining, did you?"

But once back on the island, he let himself be swept back into the easier pace of island life, capitalizing on what really mattered: basking in the company of family and friends for days at a time, remembering, through the love of family and friends, his worth and the value of his soul – and even considered the hereafter by going to church; because the island had reminded him of the one thing he had forgotten in America – Life is not always about beating the competition, or acquiring 'things,' but about savoring life in the now, with all the senses. The one who learns about the real meaning of life first, wins. He learned to once again ignore hyper-materialism, understanding that the profit one's employment yields should serve the one so employed and not a person who did not provide sweat equity. It's all about sweat equity. You should get out of life what you put in. No more. No less. "Having" is not the objective. That only leads to greed and greed is never satisfied. You could work yourself to death and never have truly lived. A man can only drive one car at a time. It is, after all, as Christ said, the soul that gives Life. Everything else profits nothing. "Being" – that was the objective. On the island, there seems to be a certain bow to the old Japanese adage, "less is more." Love your soul. And the souls of others. All the food, family co-existing, enjoying the moment one is in – these are all the color of Love. And Love is the true meaning of Life. We are told "God is Love" and "Love is of God." So simple. Yet we lose sight of it and die unsatisfied because we let go its grip on our lives. In Ikaria where God, family, food, dance, nature and music are all intertwined, it can remind us to allow it to take hold of us again.

Epilogue

SAYING GOOD-BYE

Greece is a land of magic, and of emotion, and, for me, the key to understanding myself.

As any immigrant's child, I straddled a thin, yet unmistakable line. I am an American, but not quite. I am a Greek, but not quite. Whatever family roots I may have are stranded somewhere on "the other side." And, unlike well established and settled immigrants who came here during the last three centuries, I may never know them. But I wanted to. I wanted to be in touch with my ancestors. I wanted to learn who I truly was – for an ancestor's past is the descendant's path forward. You cannot underestimate the power of self-identity.

When I boarded the jet for Greece, I was keenly aware that only Ikaria, and, more specifically, only one village, Perdiki, held any interest for me.

Perdiki, my father's hometown, is a small village owning two churches and a few houses scattered carelessly outside the main drag. When I was there, there were not many stores, but it did boast of one great area of settlement – that section of town called Lefatos.

The old Lefas house, two stories of rock, whitewashed plaster and green shutters and doors, stands more accessible than it ever has been by one wavering and unpredictable dirt road strewn with bits of broken rock. I first came down the road on Sept. 8 in the hot, windy mid-day when the sky and sea were so blue in harmony, only a thin strip of white washed blue streaming horizontally distinguished where the sea ended and the sky began.

My cousin George's red motorcycle labored down the road past wandering goats, till it could go no farther, and with my cousin leading, we left the machine against the ancient gray island rocks and jumped down that tipsy, rocky path to a still working farm house, old and defiant, where life had not been abandoned for the New World.

An old man with a sun faded blue shirt, shredded from age at the shoulder and sleeves, was working alone by a gate made of branches.

His face was aging and whisker stubs bristled from his stocky, well-shaped chin and jaws in pepper gray. His face was reddened by field work, and his broad hand, though dirt crescent around the nails and calloused at the palm, delivered a perfect gentleman's handshake. He had a weather worn smile that reflected open honesty like his eyes, and his graying hair stood up in spats and bristles where blown from the wind.

It was this gentleman, with earth worn pants and decaying shirt that exposed a hairy, sun burnt chest rounded like a house, that welcomed us. He alone was visible of all the inhabitants of Lefatos. He stood against the rocky, sparse green island hills and the blue Aegean.

When George and I finally battled our way through the bare, rocky trail where dust and rock chips kicked up hot and dry and approached that first gate that spoke of life in such a remote setting, the giant man, now a bit shrunken with age, lifted his square, strong head and squinted carefully at the two strangers through steel blue eyes.

"Hello," George called in a loud voice. "Could you please tell us where the old house of Philip Lefas is?"

"Philip Lefas?" the old man took a step closer to examine us more carefully, then cautiously added, "He is not here."

"We know," my cousin returned kindly. "He is in America. His daughter is here and wants to see the house."

"His daughter? Where is she?" he squinted all the harder.

"Here I am," I replied, stepping closer at his interest. "My father's father was George Lefas and my father is Philip. Do you know him?"

"Know him!" came the excited reply with a gusto I had not expected. "Of course I know him! Did you say you were his daughter or his grand-daughter?"

"His daughter," I smiled.

He laid down the shovel he was carrying by an outdoor stone oven and, wiping his hands against the legs of his pants, thrust one hand toward me and squinted even harder, as if the sun were in his face. His eyes searched mine for a long while, then he warmly took my hand and said with a voice, husky and soft that contained all the reminiscence of the past, "Welcome. Welcome."

I had no idea what it meant to him to have me there. He asked my name and invited us to his house. We walked a flat rock patio and from under a rock by an outdoor fireplace, he withdrew an enormous old rusty key, almost as thick as his wrist, and jabbed it into a hole in the green wooden door. It swung easily open. I never did ask why he had his door locked in such a deserted area.

Inside the house the walls were white washed plaster as outside and everything was neat and meticulously in place. The floors were wide planks of brown painted wood and the ceiling was a fixture of straight branches and stones.

"I have a picture," he said without finishing his sentence and urged me eagerly into the living room.

Before he took it off the wall where it had hung for so many years that the plaster beneath was discolored, I had recognized it. It was the army picture of my father in his uniform and a friend / cousin whose face I had grown up with, next to him. Behind the two rugged, smiling and well polished American soldiers was a painted studio background of a mountain.

I rushed at the picture. It was the first time I had seen my father's face in five months.

"You recognize your father?" he smiled as he handed me the picture.

"Of course I do," I said, looking eagerly over the picture. I was surprised that the old farmer we approached for directions would have my own father so dear to his heart.

"That's me next to him," he pointed. "Colorado Springs. Many years. Many years."

He anxiously asked how my father was doing and if I had any brothers or sisters. He asked quickly as if afraid to allow his curiosity to linger.

Outside again, we followed the man's footsteps to my father's old house, the one my grandfather had built. The shutters on the second level were closed shut. The door was locked and I had no key. I circled the house and tripped on a roughly made marble dish. I knew it was here that the house cats were fed with fresh goat's milk.

I could only see through the kitchen window. Clothes still hung on pegs in the kitchen and a broom rested in the corner. I could see where the kitchen fireplace had been blackened by use. Cobwebs blurred my view, but I could see the kitchen entrance and the absence of anything electrical was evident.

I scanned the area. Old houses left standing mute, all with the history "Occupants left for America." There was an old stone house built during the lively pirate season of the 17th century. It was hewn into a crevasse of the rock surrounding it so as to be hidden from view by pirates at sea. One of many such houses, it was so tightly closed in that even lights from within the house were not visible from the sea or close shore. But it no longer had a story to tell. I heard the old man's voice say, "And him, gone to Ohio."

My eyes scanned the seascape that lay so close to my father's deserted house. I could pick out the familiar landscapes from all my father's stories. It was as if I had, at one point, lived here myself.

And suddenly I realized that I belonged. This was my root and foundation. I touched the hot earth, smelled the salty wind as it brushed in from the sea and felt the heat of that predictable Greek sun pounding on my head – and knew that I had finally come home.

Our old friend brought us back into his house, past the goat stable my father used to clean out, and its stone roof made of flat granite slabs where my father cured the goat meat for his mother. We sat down in the kitchen where this new friend served us water and cherries in rich syrup, Glyko. I asked him to write down his name so I could take it back to my father and, after searching the house for what little paper he possessed, he laboriously scribbled his name and a few short words.

I took the paper, folded it, put it in my bag, and looked once more at my father's picture on the wall.

It was time to go now. I shook my new friend's hand warmly and followed my cousin up the path to where the motorcycle waited. I remember my father saying of this man, "We use to play together as children. We grew up together and when we came to this country, we joined the same company in the army."

I climbed the hill but took one more look. The church of St. George loomed behind us, the seascape before us where the shores of Turkey, Samos and Patmos spitted across the far away view on that warm Aegean. The old houses huddled together like forgotten widows. There were the empty courtyards and empty stables that glistened mutely under the hot sun, and the grass left to grow again, crackling dryly against the stones of the ancient, beaten paths, and the high, deep blue sky that forever remains the same – and Gustos Lefas, my father's old school mate and cousin who was more like a friend – they all belonged to the same origin, the same mark in life.

Gustos stood there waving vigorously to us. His goats bleated and brushed against his legs. His tattered shirt blew out in the mild breeze like the sails of an old ship. In his eyes I saw all that my father had left behind.

∾∾∾

LIVING (and eating), DELIBERATELY

LIVING (and eating), DELIBERATELY

Made in the USA
Middletown, DE
06 September 2023

38112225R00097